THE BAKING CLUB

bakedin

INTRO

THE BAKEDIN STORY

Hi, I'm Joe. I'm not strictly the author of this book, but I manage a little business called Bakedin, along with my brother Patrick. This book isn't just a collection of recipes. Well, technically it is, but it's actually 50 recipes that, when put together, tell a story of the making of one of the most-loved home-baking brands in the UK.

It all started back in 2013. I'd spent my entire career working for a large IT company as a software engineering manager. It was a good place to work, with a great bunch of people, but there was something missing. It took me 15 years to figure out what it was before it finally clicked: I wasn't that into computers. To give it some context, I was working on the software that runs the software that cash machines run on. To this day I'm pretty sure my Mum and Dad had no idea what I did, and if I'm being really honest, neither did I.

I'd always been passionate about food, both eating and cooking it, and longed to start my own business, leaving a string of half-started, hare-brained ideas in my wake. I used to share a lift to work with a friend, Anna, and one day during the journey we started discussing the meal kit recipe boxes that had become popular. To cut a long story short, we decided there was nothing out there giving a baking-from-scratch experience to people in the same way these other boxes did. We hatched a plan to take some of our favourite recipes and turn them into kits, with everything weighed out into just the right amounts.

Anna and I bagged up 100 of these kits and gave them to friends and family to see if they liked them. The answer was a resounding Yes! The next step was to see if people would pay for them, so along with our friend Elaina we designed some (very) basic packaging and spent an evening packing up kits into brown paper bags. Over the following weekends we set up a little stall at a few local markets and had a fantastic response – in some cases selling out. The next couple of years were a whirlwind, working at our day jobs, making kits in the evenings and selling them at weekends. We had some professional-looking labels made and started to pick up a few small stockists, many of which still sell our kits today. There were trade shows, markets, late nights, early mornings, chocolate-tasting, tears, high-fives, meeting the prime minister, Great Taste Awards, burnt samples and a lot of fun.

Fast forward to 2015, and we'd come to a crossroads in the business. The last two years of 18-hour days had taken their toll, and none of us felt we could go on in the same way whilst keeping our sanity. We had a major high-street retailer interested in stocking us, but we couldn't do it from our current production facility, and certainly not around full-time jobs. My day job was no longer motivating me to get out of bed in the morning, so the time felt right to do something about it. We knocked up a business plan which I sent around to family and friends to raise the necessary capital to hire a team and set up a better-equipped factory. Two days later I'd raised the full amount we were looking for and handed in my notice. The next chapter of the Bakedin story was ready to begin.

One of our new shareholders happened to be none other than Michel Roux OBE. Michel was introduced to me by a family friend and I practically sprinted to The Waterside Inn in Bray when I was given the opportunity to talk to him about our idea for launching the Baking Club. Never in my wildest dreams did I ever think I'd be sitting opposite one of the most significant figures in the culinary world, pitching my business idea to him. Spoiler alert: he loved it! He became a valued and enthusiastic supporter, assisting us in developing and approving our recipes.

THE BAKING CLUB

Part of the business plan was to develop the concept of a baking subscription box: a different recipe and kit sent out each month in a letterbox-sized box. It was an ambitious plan because there's a massive amount of work involved in releasing a new product every month, and building a customer base for a subscription box was more complicated than I first thought.

We set about coming up with our first few recipes to get the club off the ground. Our recipe development process is thorough – and it needs to be, because our goal was to be sending the boxes to tens of thousands of people every month. First our product development team comes up with ideas for a recipe and test-bakes a few versions that get handed out in the office for tasting. It will come as no surprise that the product development team are the most popular people in the building! We all give our feedback, and, once we have one that is a hit, the recipe then goes into the test-baking phase. Three people from the team bake it and give their feedback on the process and instructions. Once the product team are happy, it comes to Patrick or I for a final test-bake and sign-off before being sent to Michel. He'd then test the recipe, give us his feedback and changes to make the recipe even better. Once he was happy, he'd provide the seal of approval and it would be ready to go out to club members.

We launched the club with about 150 subscribers, almost exclusively family and friends. One of my favourite recipes that my mum used to make when I was growing up was a banana loaf, so we started there and added some toffee sauce on the top. It was delicious – check out page 94 for the recipe. This month we made nearly 20,000 boxes – it takes eight people an entire day just to apply the postage labels! Head over to bakedin.co.uk/book to see what it's all about and for a little discount off your first box.

A FAMILY BUSINESS

My brother Patrick had recently left the army and was running his own personal training business in his spare time while working for the Ministry of Defence during the day. Trying to run the Bakedin business alone was taking its toll on me so Patrick came on board as a director as Head of Sales. He built a small sales team and used a little of the powers of persuasion he'd learned in the army to convince retailers to give our kits a go. At the time of writing we've now got products in more than 1,000 shops across the UK and some ambitious plans to take the brand worldwide. At first our Mum was slightly concerned about us joining forces because as kids we spent most of our time together in fierce battles, either on the tennis court or over computer games. However, when we're working on the same team rather than competing, it seems to work well and it's been great to share the highs and lows together.

THE FUTURE

I'm writing this in August 2020. Earlier this year we were given the heartbreaking news that Michel Roux had passed away, surrounded by his family. He will be fondly remembered by everyone at Bakedin as a funny, generous and inspirational man. I'll never forget visiting him at his house in St Tropez for a photo shoot for the Baking Club and having lunch with his family on his patio. Last year Patrick and I had lunch with him at The Waterside Inn, and it was without doubt the best meal I've ever had. I know he loved the Baking Club and was proud of what we built together. It's also been a strange year for the entire world with a lot of lives dramatically affected by the Covid-19 pandemic, but one of the positive things to come about during lockdown was that the nation's love of baking was taken to a new level. Our tagline is 'Happiness is Homemade' and this began to resonate with more families as they discovered how rewarding baking at home can be. The Baking Club has grown enormously this year, to the point we've had to get new premises (our fourth since starting the business) and the team has now grown to nearly 50 people. We've just launched a new subscription, the Bread Baking Club, so maybe this will be the first book of many.

So, there you have it. It's been a rollercoaster ride over the last seven years, with way more highs than lows, and this recipe book marks an important milestone in our history. I hope you will love these recipes as much as our members have, and I look forward to seeing you in the club!

– Joe and the Bakedin team

ABOUT THIS BOOK

When we first launched the Baking Club, we had a goal of using recipes that were accessible to novice bakers but also creative and interesting enough to allow more experienced bakers to add their own spin and build up their baking repertoire. To this end, we designed the recipes so you'll only ever need five types of tin to make them: a round tin, square tin, loaf tin, baking tray and a muffin tin. We split this recipe book into sections that match up with these tins, all of which are readily available (we even sell a starter bundle at bakedin.co.uk). The Bakedin team have voted, and the consensus is these are the recipes you should try first:

- Round Tin: Raspberry Ripple Cake (page 41)
- Baking Tray: Soft Pretzels (page 62)
- Square Tin: Chocolate and Pecan Millionaire Squares (page 80)
- Loaf Tin: Sticky Toffee and Ginger Loaf (page 101)
- Muffin Tin: Blueberry Muffins (page 112)

If you like the recipes in this book, then you'll love our Baking Club. We send our members a brand new recipe and baking kit through their letterbox every month. You get access to all the past recipes and can join our thriving online community sharing photos, baking tips and making baking besties. Head over to bakedin.co.uk/book to see what it's all about, join the club and to get an exclusive discount for owners of this book.

BASINGSTOKE
PM
5 OCT
2020

ROUND TIN RECIPES

GINGERBREAD LATTE CAKE

Inspired by a festive coffee shop favourite, this is a stunning four-layer winter-spiced ginger sponge cake. Each layer is drizzled with coffee syrup, then sandwiched with coffee-flavoured Swiss meringue buttercream. The cake is lightly iced with more Swiss meringue buttercream to give a naked effect. Decorate with a snowflake template, dust with cinnamon sugar and you have a wonderful centrepiece for your Christmas table.

Serves 16

180ml milk
1 tablespoon lemon juice
180g unsalted butter,
  softened
100g caster sugar, plus
  1 extra teaspoon
75g dark brown sugar
295g self-raising flour
1 tablespoon ground ginger
1 teaspoon baking powder
2 teaspoons ground
  cinnamon
½ teaspoon ground
  nutmeg
½ teaspoon ground
  mixed spice
½ teaspoon fine salt
3 medium eggs

For the coffee syrup
5g coffee granules
30g granulated sugar
4 tablespoons boiling water

Preheat the oven to 180°C/160°C fan/gas mark 4. Grease the tins and line with circles of baking paper. If you do not have four tins, you will need to bake in batches, using a fresh circle of baking paper each time.

Pour the milk into a bowl and stir in the lemon juice. Set aside to sour (it should thicken and curdle slightly).

In a large bowl, beat the butter, 100g caster sugar and the dark brown sugar together for a few minutes until light and fluffy. Add the flour, ginger, baking powder, 1 teaspoon of cinnamon, the nutmeg, mixed spice and salt into the butter mixture, along with the eggs and sour milk. Give everything a good mix until well combined.

Divide the mixture evenly between the four prepared tins, level off and bake for 18–20 minutes, until a skewer inserted into the centre comes out clean.

Leave the cakes to cool in their tins for 10–15 minutes while you prepare the coffee syrup. Put the coffee and sugar in a heatproof bowl with the boiling water. Stir until the coffee and sugar have dissolved. Turn the cakes out of their tins and discard the baking paper. With the bottom of the sponges facing upwards, brush or drizzle the coffee syrup over each of the four sponges, reserving 1 tablespoon of syrup for later.

For the icing, put the egg whites in a clean, heatproof bowl. Add the caster sugar and whisk until combined. Position the bowl over a pan of gently simmering water, being careful that the bowl does not touch the water. Whisk the mixture until the sugar has completely dissolved and is no longer grainy; this should take around 2–3 minutes. If it still feels grainy (test by rubbing a small amount between your thumb and finger), keep whisking until smooth. Take the bowl off the pan (be careful as it will be hot) and continue whisking for 10–15 minutes, until the mixture feels stiffer and is no longer warm to the touch. Whisk the cubed butter into the mixture

For the icing

2 medium egg whites
130g caster sugar
220g unsalted butter,
   cubed and softened

You will need

1 x 18cm round cake tins
baking paper
snowflake template/stencil

bit by bit until smooth. Add the remaining coffee syrup and stir to combine. The icing may look a little lumpy, but if you keep whisking it will become smooth.

Start assembling the cake by placing one sponge on a plate and adding 2–3 heaped tablespoons of icing, spreading it evenly across the top. Position the next sponge on top and spread the same amount of icing onto this. Repeat this process with the other sponges. When you reach the final sponge, spread the icing over the top and around the sides of the cake. Scrape quite close to the edges to create a 'naked layer' effect. Put the cake in the fridge to chill for 20 minutes.

Position the stencil onto the cooled cake and, using a sieve, dust the remaining teaspoon of cinnamon and 1 teaspoon of caster sugar over it, then remove the stencil very carefully to reveal the pattern. Try not to drop any of the cinnamon mixture off the stencil as you lift it, as this will interfere with your pattern.

ORANGE & CARDAMOM CAKE

A delicately scented polenta, orange and cardamom cake, sandwiched and topped with a subtle orange-flavoured, tangy cream cheese icing. The aromatic warmth of the cardamom gives this citrusy bake an unusal twist to liven up this teatime treat.

Serves 8

190g self-raising flour
½ teaspoon baking powder
½ teaspoon bicarbonate
  of soda
50g polenta
⅛ teaspoon ground
  cardamom
100g caster sugar
100g soft light brown sugar
grated zest and juice
  of 1 orange
225g unsalted butter,
  softened
4 large eggs

For the icing
190g cream cheese
350g icing sugar
25g unsalted butter

You will need
2 x 18cm round cake tins
baking paper

Preheat the oven to 180°C/160°C fan/gas mark 4. Lightly grease the cake tins and line with circles of baking paper.

In a large bowl, combine the flour, baking powder, bicarbonate of soda, polenta and cardamom. Stir through the sugars, orange zest and half the orange juice, then mix in the butter and eggs, beating with a spoon until light and fluffy.

Divide the cake batter evenly between the prepared tins. Bake for 20–25 minutes, until golden in colour and a skewer inserted into the centre comes out clean. Leave the cakes to cool for 5 minutes in the tins before transferring to a wire rack to cool completely.

While the cakes are cooling, prepare the icing. In a large bowl, combine the cream cheese with the icing sugar and butter. Add the remaining orange juice, and beat together until stiff and smooth. Chill in the fridge for 10 minutes.

Ensuring both cakes are completely cool, turn one of the cakes so it sits bottom-side-up on a plate and remove the baking paper. Spread half the icing evenly over the top of the cake, then lightly sandwich the second cake on top and spread the remaining icing neatly over the top of the cake.

TOP TIP
Add a little orange zest to the icing for a more intense citrus flavour.

STICKY TOFFEE DRIP CAKE

A tasty two-layered sticky toffee and date sponge, sandwiched together with a light, sweet buttercream and iced to give a naked effect. The cake is very generously smothered with a gleaming toffee sauce, creating a tempting drip around the edges. Try not to eat this all at once…

Serves 12

210g chopped dates
1 teaspoon bicarbonate
  of soda
3 medium eggs
145g soft light brown sugar
120g unsalted butter,
  melted and cooled
200g self-raising flour
pinch of salt

For the icing

120g unsalted butter,
  softened
200g icing sugar
1 tablespoon milk

For the toffee sauce

45g unsalted butter
110g demerara sugar
110ml double cream

You will need

2 x 18cm round cake tins
baking paper

Preheat the oven to 180°C/160°C fan/gas mark 4. Grease each tin with a little butter and line both tins with circles of baking paper.

Put the chopped dates and bicarbonate of soda in a pan with 130ml of water and bring to the boil, stirring gently. Remove from the heat and stir for another minute, then set aside.

In a large bowl, beat together the eggs and light brown sugar for about 5 minutes. Stir in the melted butter and gently mix in the dates, then fold the flour and salt into the mixture.

Divide the batter equally between the prepared tins, level the mixture off, then bake in the oven for 25 minutes or until a skewer inserted into the centre of each cake comes out clean. Leave to cool completely in their tins, then turn out onto a wire rack.

While the cakes are cooling, make the icing. Beat together the butter, icing sugar and milk until smooth. Spread one-third of the icing over one of the sponges and sandwich with the other sponge. Put the cake on a plate and spread the rest of the icing over the cake, scraping close to the edges to create a 'naked layer' effect. Put the cake in the fridge to chill.

Before starting the toffee sauce, make sure you have all the ingredients you need to hand. Put the butter and demerara sugar in a saucepan over a low heat. Let the butter melt slightly then add the double cream and stir continuously. Be careful as the sauce will be hot. When the mixture has combined and the sugar has dissolved, turn the heat up slightly, continuing to stir. Let the sauce bubble for 3 minutes until it has thickened. Take off the heat and stir for a few seconds, then pour the toffee sauce into a heatproof jug and set aside to cool.

Once the toffee sauce has cooled, remove the cake from the fridge and transfer to a plate or cake stand. Give the sauce a little stir, then start drizzling it over the cake. Use a knife to help smooth it towards the edges and let it drizzle down the sides to create the desired drip effect.

TOP TIP
If the toffee sauce has not cooled enough, the sauce will run off the edges of the cake. However, if left to cool for too long, the sauce will set and won't create the drip effect, so keep an eye on it!

CHOCOLATE HONEYCOMB CAKE

A rich, two-layered, dark chocolate cake sandwiched together with a thick buttercream filling and iced with a glossy chocolate ganache. This showstopping cake is topped with fragments of honeycomb, giving a deliciously crunchy texture.

Serves 10–12

50g dark chocolate
200g unsalted butter, softened
200g soft light brown sugar
3 medium eggs
200ml milk
170g self-raising flour
50g cocoa powder
½ teaspoon baking powder
40g honeycomb, smashed into different-sized pieces

For the buttercream
80g unsalted butter, softened
100g icing sugar
20g cocoa powder
1 tablespoon milk

For the chocolate ganache
15g unsalted butter
1 tablespoon milk
15g icing sugar
50g dark chocolate

You will need
2 x 18cm round cake tins
baking paper

Preheat the oven to 180°C/160°C fan/gas mark 4. Grease each tin with a little butter and line both tins with circles of baking paper.

Break the dark chocolate into a heatproof bowl set over a pan of gently simmering water, ensuring the bowl does not touch the water. Once melted, set aside to cool.

In a large bowl, cream together the butter and light brown sugar until light and fluffy. Add the melted chocolate, beating again to incorporate.

Beat the eggs and milk in a jug. In a separate bowl, combine the flour, cocoa powder and baking powder. Add half the egg and milk mixture to the creamed butter and chocolate mixture and fold in gently. Then fold in half the dry ingredients, and repeat these steps until both are used up and the mixture is smooth.

Divide the mixture evenly between the two prepared tins and bake for 30–35 minutes, or until a skewer inserted into the centre of each comes out with just a few crumbs. Let the cakes cool in the tins for 10 minutes before turning out onto a wire rack to cool completely.

To make the buttercream filling, cream the butter with the icing sugar and cocoa powder until smooth. Add 1 tablespoon of milk and beat for a minute or two until you have a fluffy filling.

Turn one of the cake layers upside-down on a cake stand or plate and spread the buttercream filling evenly, sandwiching it with the second layer.

To make the chocolate ganache, heat the butter with 1 tablespoon of milk in a pan until steaming. Add the icing sugar and chocolate and stir until the chocolate is melted and you have a glossy, smooth icing. Leave to cool for 10–15 minutes, or until it is thick enough to spread.

Spread the cooled ganache over the top of the cake and leave to set for 10–15 minutes. Sprinkle over the honeycomb just before serving.

RASPBERRY & CHOCOLATE CAKE

A beautiful, three-layered, chocolate sponge cake with a delicious chocolate filling. The cake is iced with a tasty raspberry buttercream and topped with fresh raspberries and a sprinkling of dark chocolate curls. This cake is just perfect to bring out on a special occasion.

Serves 12

5 medium eggs
180g caster sugar
95g self-raising flour
45g cocoa powder
145g unsalted butter,
 melted and cooled
2 teaspoons dark
 chocolate curls
50g raspberries

For the raspberry syrup
100g raspberries
75g granulated sugar

For the chocolate filling
100g dark chocolate chips
50g unsalted butter, cubed

For the raspberry buttercream
115g unsalted butter,
 softened
150g icing sugar

You will need
3 x 18cm round cake tins
baking paper

Preheat the oven to 180°C/160°C fan/gas mark 4. Grease the cake tins and line with circles of baking paper. If you do not have three tins, you will need to bake in batches, using a fresh circle of baking paper each time.

Break the eggs into a large bowl and add the sugar. Whisk together for 5–10 minutes, until the mixture is thick and nearly doubled in volume. Add the flour and cocoa powder and gently fold together. Drizzle the melted butter over the top of the mixture and gently fold in. Make sure the butter and flour are fully combined, but be careful not to over mix as you do not want to knock too much air out of the mixture.

Divide the cake mixture evenly between the prepared tins and bake for 15–20 minutes, or until a skewer inserted into the centre of each cake comes out clean. Leave the cakes in their tins on a wire rack for 10–15 minutes to cool. Run a knife around the edge of the cakes to loosen, then transfer to the wire rack to cool completely.

While the cakes are cooling, make the raspberry syrup. Put the raspberries, sugar and 50ml of water into a saucepan. Bring to the boil, then lower the heat and simmer gently for around 10 minutes, stirring frequently. When the syrup has thickened slightly, strain the mixture through a sieve into a clean bowl to remove any seeds (discard the seeds). Leave to cool completely.

For the chocolate filling, position a heatproof bowl over a pan of gently simmering water, ensuring the bowl does not touch the water. Put the chocolate chips in the bowl with the butter and stir together until melted. Carefully remove the bowl from the pan and continue to stir for a minute until it cools slightly. Leave to cool at room temperature for 15–20 minutes, or until it has started to thicken.

For the raspberry buttercream, put the butter in a bowl and beat for a minute to soften. Gradually add the icing sugar along with 1½ tablespoons of the raspberry syrup; if you prefer a darker shade of pink, add an extra tablespoon of syrup. Beat everything together until soft and fluffy.

Start to assemble the cake. Be gentle with the sponges as they will be quite delicate. Put one sponge on a plate or cake stand and spread half the chocolate filling over, leaving a 0.5cm gap around the outer edge of the cake. Put the second sponge on top and repeat, finishing with the final sponge on top. Ice the sides and top of the cake with the raspberry buttercream. Finally, decorate with the dark chocolate curls and raspberries. Slide a fork up the edge of the cake to create a pattern in the buttercream.

TOP TIP
Clean your palette knife or spatula after each application of buttercream to prevent the crumbs spreading into the icing.

TRIPLE CHOCOLATE FUDGE CAKE

A sumptuous two-layered dark chocolate sponge cake sandwiched together with sweet, chocolatey whipped cream, mixed with chocolate chips. The cake is iced with a decadent dark chocolate ganache. For a spooky Halloween finish, try the cobweb effect on top.

Serves 12

3 tablespoons cocoa
   powder
5 tablespoons hot water
3 medium eggs
200g unsalted butter,
   softened
200g self-raising flour
1 teaspoon baking powder
200g caster sugar

For the filling
150ml double cream
1 tablespoon cocoa
   powder
50g icing sugar
30g milk chocolate chips

For the icing
100g dark chocolate
150ml double cream
50g white chocolate

You will need
2 x 18cm round cake tins
baking paper

Preheat the oven to 180°C/160°C fan/gas mark 4. Grease each tin with a little butter and line both tins with circles of baking paper.

Put the cocoa powder in a small bowl. Add the hot water and mix until smooth.

Put the eggs, butter, flour, baking powder and sugar in a large bowl and beat well. Stir in the cocoa mixture until you have a smooth cake batter.

Divide the mixture equally between the two prepared tins. Bake the cakes for 20–25 minutes. Check they are done by lightly pressing your finger onto a sponge. If it bounces back it's done. Leave to cool completely in the tins then run a knife around the edges of the tins to loosen and turn them out.

For the filling, whip the double cream in a bowl until stiff, then stir in the cocoa powder, icing sugar and milk chocolate chips. Spread the filling over one of the cake layers, then carefully position the other layer on top. Put the cake in the fridge to firm up while you make the icing.

For the icing, put the dark chocolate in a heatproof bowl over a pan of gently simmering water, ensuring the bowl doesn't touch the water. Add the double cream and stir until smooth and melted together. Very carefully remove the bowl from the pan and stir for a couple of minutes to cool slightly. Put in the fridge for 30 minutes to firm up.

Spread the chocolate icing over the top of the cake, then spread a thin layer over the sides.

Melt the white chocolate in a heatproof bowl over a pan of gently simmering water, ensuring the bowl doesn't touch the water. Leave to cool slightly, then drizzle the white chocolate in a circle in the centre of the cake (use a piping bag if necessary). Add more circles around it, then drag a skewer through the circles from the centre to the edge to create a cobweb pattern, or experiment with your own designs.

LOTUS BISCOFF, CARAMEL, CHOCOLATE & WALNUT TART

For a truly decadent dessert, try this delightfully gooey tart. The delicate pastry case is filled with a thick caramel sauce, crunchy chopped walnuts, and topped with a rich chocolate layer. The tart is finished with a generous drizzle of caramel sauce and a crisp sprinkle of crushed Lotus Biscoff biscuits.

Serves 8–10

For the pastry
125g plain flour
25g icing sugar
75g unsalted butter,
  cubed, at room
  temperature
1 egg yolk

For the caramel sauce
50g caster sugar
15g soft light brown sugar
¼ teaspoon salt
25g unsalted butter
40g Lotus Biscoff spread
150ml double cream

For the chocolate filling
2 eggs
50g caster sugar
½ tablespoon cocoa
  powder
75g dark chocolate chips
50g unsalted butter
20g walnuts, chopped

To make the pastry, put the flour and icing sugar in a bowl with the butter and use your fingers to rub the mixture together until you have a breadcrumb-like consistency. Add the egg yolk and bring the pastry together using a wooden spoon, then use your hands to shape it into a ball. Turn the pastry out onto your worktop and knead gently for 30 seconds until smooth. If the pastry feels very soft, wrap it in cling film and put it in the fridge for about 15 minutes.

Grease the cake tin and line with a circle of baking paper. Unwrap the chilled pastry and put it onto another sheet of baking paper on the work surface. Roll out until 0.5cm thick and around 3cm wider than the cake tin. Gently lift the paper and flip the pastry into the tin, then discard the paper. Gently press the pastry onto the base of the tin and into the edges. Cut off the excess pastry, leaving a 1cm overhang around the edge. Prick the base of the tart all over with a fork then put the tin into the fridge for at least 15 minutes to firm up.

Before starting the caramel sauce, make sure you have all the ingredients you need for this step to hand. Put the sugars and salt in a saucepan with 30ml of water and gently stir, then position over a medium heat and bring to the boil. You will need to stir occasionally to stop the mixture burning at the edges. You are aiming for a deep amber-coloured syrup, which should take about 3–5 minutes. Take the pan off the heat and stir in the butter (this mixture will be extremely hot), and once the butter has melted, stir in the Lotus Biscoff spread. Return the pan to a medium heat, stir in the double cream and bring back to the boil, stirring all the time. Take the caramel sauce off the heat, transfer to a clean bowl and set aside.

To make the chocolate filling, position a heatproof bowl over a saucepan of gently simmering water, ensuring the water does not touch the bowl. Add the eggs and caster sugar to the bowl and whisk continuously for around 5 minutes, until you have a thickened, foamy mixture. Remove the bowl from the saucepan (be careful as it will be hot) and continue whisking, off the heat, for another 3 minutes. The mixture will slowly continue to thicken as it cools. Briefly fold through the cocoa powder and set aside.

Put the chocolate chips and butter in a clean, heatproof bowl over a pan of simmering water, stirring occasionally until both have melted and combined into a smooth mixture. Leave to cool for a few minutes, then gently and gradually fold the egg mixture into the chocolate mixture until you have a chocolate-mousse-like consistency.

Preheat the oven to 180°C/160°C fan/gas mark 4. Take the pastry case out of the fridge, spoon three-quarters of the caramel sauce into the case and smooth evenly across the bottom. Scatter the chopped walnuts evenly over the caramel sauce, then spoon the chocolate mixture over the top and level. Tap the tin on your work surface a couple of times to remove any large air pockets, then bake for 25–30 minutes, until the top is crisp and the tart filling doesn't wobble when shaken.

Remove the tart from the oven and leave to cool in the tin for at least 30 minutes or until cool to the touch. Remove from the tin. Add the icing sugar to the remaining caramel sauce and stir until you have a smooth icing. Drizzle this over the tart and finish with a sprinkling of the Lotus Biscoff crumb. The tart is best served chilled.

RASPBERRY ETON MESS CAKE

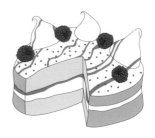

For a fun, flavourful take on the classic Victoria sponge, try this golden, light sponge cake, filled and topped with a sweet raspberry syrup, whipped cream, crispy meringues and a sprinkle of tart raspberry pieces. An impressive addition to any summer picnic.

Serves 12

150g unsalted butter, softened
100g caster sugar
3 medium eggs
150g self-raising flour
5g baking powder
300ml double cream
2.5g freeze-dried raspberries
30g raspberries

For the meringues
60g caster sugar
small pinch of salt
1 medium egg white

For the raspberry syrup
110g raspberries
75g caster sugar

You will need
2 x 18cm round cake tins
baking paper
baking tray
small piping bag

Preheat the oven to 180°C/160°C fan/gas mark 4. Grease each tin with a little butter and line both tins with circles of baking paper.

In a large bowl, beat together the butter and sugar for a few minutes until light and fluffy. Add the eggs, flour and baking powder and continue to beat until the mixture is smooth.

Divide the batter evenly between the prepared tins and level off the mixture. Bake for 18–22 minutes until the cakes are well risen and a skewer inserted into the centre of each comes out clean. Leave to cool in the tins for a few minutes, then turn out onto a wire rack to cool completely.

Reduce the oven temperature to 120°C/100°C fan/gas mark ½. For the meringues, line a baking tray with a sheet of baking paper. Combine the sugar and salt in a small bowl. Put the egg white in a clean bowl and whisk until soft peaks form. Still whisking, add 1 tablespoon at a time of the sugar and salt until the mixture becomes thick and glossy and the sugar has dissolved. Check by rubbing a small amount between your fingers – if it is grainy, continue to whisk for a couple more minutes.

Transfer the mixture to the piping bag and cut 3cm off the end of the bag. Pipe eight small peaked swirls onto the lined baking tray, keeping them as even as possible. Put the meringues into the oven and reduce the temperature again to 110°C/90°C fan/gas mark ¼. Bake for 60–70 minutes until firm to the touch. Turn off the oven and allow the meringues to cool inside the oven for 30–45 minutes; this helps them remain crisp on the outside and soft in the middle.

While the meringues are cooling, make the raspberry syrup. Put the raspberries, sugar and 50ml of water in a saucepan. Bring to the boil, then lower the heat and simmer gently for around 10 minutes. When the syrup has thickened slightly, strain the mixture through a sieve into a clean bowl to remove any seeds (discard the seeds). Leave to cool completely.

When the meringues, sponges and syrup are cool, you are ready to assemble the cake. First whip the cream to form soft peaks, being careful not to over whip. Using half of the raspberry syrup, drizzle it over both sponges, spreading it evenly. Spread half the whipped cream over one of the sponges and roughly level off. Using half of the remaining syrup, drizzle directly over the cream and use a fork to swirl it around. On top of the cream, arrange 4 of the meringues, half the freeze-dried raspberries and a few of the fresh raspberries.

Take the second sponge and put it raspberry-syrup-side-down on the other sponge. Add the remaining whipped cream, raspberries and meringues to the top of your cake. Finish by drizzling over the remaining raspberry syrup and scattering over the last of the freeze-dried raspberries.

TOP TIP
If you find you have slightly over whipped your cream, add a couple of teaspoons of milk to make it smooth again.

RASPBERRY & ALMOND CAKE

A delicious and light almond sponge cake filled with a sweet raspberry jam, smothered with a glossy white icing and topped with fragrant toasted almonds. A delightfully simple yet sensational bake.

Serves 8–10

200g unsalted butter, softened
200g caster sugar
100g ground almonds
100g self-raising flour
¼ teaspoon salt
1 teaspoon baking powder
4 large eggs
130g raspberry jam
150g icing sugar
30g toasted flaked almonds

You will need
2 x 18cm round cake tins
baking paper

Preheat the oven to 180°C/160°C fan/gas mark 4. Grease each tin with a little butter and line both tins with circles of baking paper.

In a large bowl, cream together the butter and sugar until light and fluffy. Add the ground almonds, flour, salt, baking powder and eggs and beat well.

Divide the mixture evenly between the prepared tins, smoothing the tops of the mixture with a spoon to ensure they are level. Bake for 25 minutes, or until a skewer inserted into the centre of the cakes comes out clean.

Allow the cakes to cool a little in the tins before turning out onto a wire rack. Once cool, spread the top of one cake with the jam and sandwich the other one on top.

Put the icing sugar in a bowl and gradually add 30ml of water, stirring until the mixture is thick and smooth. Spread the icing over the cake, allowing some to drip down the sides. Sprinkle the top with the toasted almonds and allow the icing to set before serving.

TOP TIP
Use cherry jam instead of raspberry and top with cherries for a tasty twist on the traditional Bakewell tart.

CHOCOLATE ORANGE MARBLE CAKE

To add a bit of zest to your day, why not try this eye-catching bake? Chocolate and orange sponge cakes are marbled together and brushed with orange syrup. The sponges are sandwiched and topped with two flavours of buttercream then decorated with a sprinkle of chocolate curls.

Serves 12

220g unsalted butter,
   softened
190g caster sugar
4 medium eggs
220g self-raising flour
grated zest of 1 orange,
   plus 1 tablespoon
   orange juice
20g cocoa powder
2½ tablespoons milk
2 teaspoons marbled
   chocolate curls

For the syrup
2 tablespoons orange juice
20g caster sugar

For the icing
160g unsalted butter,
   softened
190g icing sugar
1 teaspoon orange juice
50g dark chocolate chips

You will need
2 x 18cm round cake tins
2 small piping bags
baking paper

Preheat the oven to 180°C/160°C fan/gas mark 4. Grease the cake tins and line with circles of baking paper.

Beat the butter in a bowl for a minute or two to soften. Add the sugar and beat until light and fluffy; this may take around 5 minutes. Separate half the mixture in another bowl – there should be roughly 190g of mixture in each bowl. In one of the bowls, beat in 2 eggs, 120g self-raising flour and the orange zest. Add 1 tablespoon of orange juice to the mixture containing the zest and give it a mix until smooth.

In the second bowl of mixture, beat in the remaining eggs and self-raising flour with the cocoa powder and milk.

Put alternate spoonfuls of each mixture in the prepared cake tins, trying to make sure you have equal amounts in each. When you have used up both mixtures, give the tins a few sharp taps on your work surface to even the surfaces, then run a skewer through the cake mixture to create a swirl pattern.

Bake for 20–30 minutes, until a skewer inserted in the centre of each sponge comes out clean. Put the tins on a wire rack to cool for 5–10 minutes, then carefully turn the cakes out of the tins onto the rack so the sponges sit upside-down, as this will help keep them flat. Remove the baking paper and gently pierce the sponges with a fork.

For the syrup, combine 2 tablespoons of orange juice with the caster sugar. Brush or drizzle over the warm sponges, then leave to cool completely.

For the icing, put the butter in a bowl and beat until soft. Add the icing sugar and mix until light and fluffy. Separate half the icing in another bowl – there should be roughly 170g in each bowl. In one of the bowls, add 1 teaspoon of orange juice and mix to combine.

Melt the dark chocolate chips in a heatproof bowl over a pan of simmering water, making sure the bowl does not touch the water. Stir gently until the chocolate has melted, then leave to cool slightly. Add the melted chocolate to the second bowl of icing and combine until smooth. If your icings are a little soft, firm them up in the fridge for 5 minutes then stir again.

Position one of the cooled sponges onto a plate or serving board. Put the two different icings in two separate piping bags and snip 3cm off the ends. Using one of the bags of icing, pipe a drop in the middle of the sponge. Then use the other bag to pipe a different drop next to it. Continue to pipe the icing from alternate piping bags until you have covered the sponge.

Top with the other sponge and repeat the icing process for the top of the cake, this time making a ring of swirls around the edge of the cake, leaving the marble effect visible in the centre. Finish with a sprinkle of marbled chocolate curls.

SOUR CREAM & CHOCOLATE CAKE

A luxurious, flavourful, two-layered cake filled with a dark chocolate sour cream filling. The cake is iced with a sour cream-based buttercream, with a naked finish. For decoration, the cake is topped with a ring of dark chocolate curls, but also offers the perfect base to customise with your own decorations.

Serves 12

120g unsalted butter, softened
130g caster sugar
3 medium eggs
70g dark chocolate chips
135g self-raising flour
10g cocoa powder
½ teaspoon bicarbonate of soda
100ml sour cream
2 teaspoons dark chocolate curls, to decorate

For the filling
70g dark chocolate chips
70ml sour cream

For the buttercream
95g unsalted butter, softened
130g icing sugar
30ml sour cream

You will need
2 x 18cm round cake tins
baking paper

Preheat the oven to 180°C/160°C fan/gas mark 4. Grease each tin with a little butter and line both tins with circles of baking paper.

In a large bowl, beat the butter and caster sugar for a few minutes until light and fluffy, then beat in the eggs one at a time.

Melt the dark chocolate in a heatproof bowl set over a pan of gently simmering water, ensuring that the bowl does not touch the water. Very carefully remove the bowl from the pan and leave to cool slightly.

Add the melted chocolate to the mixture along with the flour, cocoa powder, bicarbonate of soda and sour cream, and combine everything together until smooth.

Divide the mixture equally between the two prepared tins and bake for 20–25 minutes until well risen and a skewer inserted into the centre of the cakes comes out clean. Leave to cool in the tins, then run a knife around the edge of the tins to loosen and turn the sponges out.

For the filling, put the dark chocolate and sour cream in a heatproof bowl set over a pan of gently simmering water, ensuring that the bowl does not touch the water. Stir until melted, then carefully remove the bowl from the pan and leave to cool at room temperature.

Make the buttercream by beating together the butter, icing sugar and sour cream in a bowl until smooth.

Spread the chocolate filling over one sponge and put the other sponge on top. Spread the buttercream around the top and sides of the cake. You can use a palette knife or a spatula to scrape closely to the sides to create the 'naked layer' effect. Finish by scattering the dark chocolate curls over the top of the cake to decorate.

CHOCOLATE DRIP CAKE

For the ultimate temptation, try this beautiful chocolate drip cake. An elegant, three-layer chocolate sponge sandwiched together with a toffee-flavoured buttercream icing. The dark chocolate drip gives this cake a rich flavour and perfectly complements the sweetness of the buttercream. This makes a decadent celebration cake and can be embellished however you choose.

Serves 12

27g cocoa powder
5 tablespoons hot water
200g unsalted butter,
　at room temperature
3 medium eggs
200g self-raising flour
1 teaspoon baking powder
175g caster sugar
3 tablespoons milk
2 teaspoons caramel curls

For the toffee sauce
25g unsalted butter
55g demerara sugar
55ml double cream

For the icing
180g unsalted butter,
　at room temperature
300g icing sugar

For the ganache
30g dark chocolate
70ml double cream

You will need
3 x 18cm round cake tins
baking paper
small piping bag

Preheat the oven to 180°C/160°C fan/gas mark 4. Grease the cake tins with a little butter and line with circles of baking paper. If you do not have three tins, you will need to bake in batches, using a fresh circle of baking paper each time.

Put the cocoa powder in a small bowl. Add the hot water and mix until smooth.

In a large bowl, beat together the butter, eggs, flour, baking powder and sugar. Add the cocoa mixture and milk and stir until you have a smooth batter.

Divide the batter evenly between the three cake tins. Bake for 20–25 minutes, until a skewer inserted into the centre of the cakes comes out clean. Leave to cool completely in the tin.

While the cakes are cooling, make the toffee sauce. Put the butter and demerara sugar in a saucepan over a low heat. Let the butter melt slightly, then add the double cream and stir continuously (be careful as the sauce will be hot). When everything has combined and the sugar has dissolved, turn the heat up slightly, continuing to stir. Let the sauce bubble for 1 minute, or until it has thickened, then remove from the heat and stir for a few seconds. Pour the toffee sauce into a heatproof bowl and leave to cool.

Once the cakes and toffee sauce are cool, make the toffee buttercream icing. Briefly beat the butter to soften, then gradually add the icing sugar, mixing until pale and smooth. Give the cooled toffee sauce a stir, add it to the icing, and beat until combined.

To assemble the cake, position one sponge centrally on a plate or board and spread over 2–3 tablespoons of the icing. Sandwich the second sponge on top and ice as before. Add the final sponge and, using half of the remaining icing, spread a thin layer around the sides and top of the cake (this is the crumb coat). Chill the cake in the fridge for 15–20 minutes until firm to the touch. Cover again with the remaining icing using a palette knife to smooth, and refrigerate again.

To make the chocolate ganache, break the dark chocolate into a heatproof bowl set over a pan of gently simmering water, ensuring that the bowl does not touch the water. Add the double cream and stir until smooth and combined. Remove from the heat and let the ganache cool for 5 minutes, stirring occasionally. Don't leave it for too long or it will be too firm to drip.

Transfer the ganache to the piping bag and snip 2cm off the end. Remove the chilled cake from the fridge and pipe the ganache around the top edge, letting it drip to different lengths down the sides. Pipe the remaining ganache over the centre of the cake, spreading it with a palette knife or spoon to smooth the top. Decorate with the caramel curls and chill the cake in the fridge again for 45 minutes, or until ready to serve. Allow the cake to return to room temperature before serving.

RASPBERRY RIPPLE CAKE

A light, refreshing summer bake. This is an enticing sponge cake, filled with mascarpone icing and a vibrant homemade raspberry jam. A beautifully speedy bake to make and enjoy on a blazing hot day. Have fun marbling the patterns on top of this cake.

Serves 12

195g unsalted butter, softened
130g caster sugar
4 medium eggs
195g self-raising flour
1 teaspoon baking powder
2.5g freeze-dried raspberries, to decorate

For the jam
120g raspberries
75g granulated sugar

For the icing
350g mascarpone
130g icing sugar

You will need
3 x 18cm round cake tins
baking paper

Preheat the oven to 180°C/160°C fan/gas mark 4. Grease the cake tins with a little butter and line with circles of baking paper. If you do not have three tins, you will need to bake in batches, using a fresh circle of baking paper each time.

In a large bowl, beat together the butter and sugar until light and fluffy. Add the eggs, flour and baking powder, and continue to beat until the mixture is smooth.

Divide the mixture evenly between the three prepared tins and smooth the tops using a palette knife or the back of a spoon. Bake for 18–25 minutes, or until golden and well risen and a skewer inserted into the centre of each cake comes out clean. Leave to cool in the tins for a few minutes, then turn out onto a wire rack and leave to cool completely.

While the cakes are baking, make the jam. Put the raspberries, granulated sugar and 70ml of water in a saucepan. Bring to the boil, then lower the heat and simmer for around 20–25 minutes. When the jam has thickened slightly, strain the mixture through a sieve into a clean bowl to remove any seeds (discard the seeds). Leave the jam to cool completely.

For the icing, briefly beat the mascarpone in a bowl, then gradually add the icing sugar and mix until well combined.

Once the cake layers are cool, assemble the cake. Position one of the sponges on a plate and spread it with 2 heaped tablespoons of mascarpone icing. Dollop a third of the jam over the icing, and swirl the jam into the icing. Put the second sponge on top and repeat.

Put the final sponge on top and spread a generous amount of icing over the top of the cake. Scrape a thin layer of icing around the sides of the cake using a palette knife. Dollop the remaining jam over the top of the cake and swirl carefully to achieve a distinctive ripple effect. To finish, decorate with the freeze-dried raspberries. Store in an airtight container in the fridge, and allow the cake to come back to room temperature before serving.

BAKEWELL TART

Who can resist the delicate taste of frangipane? This tart has a beautifully light, buttery pastry base, and is chock-full of sweet raspberry jam and fragrant frangipane. Decorate with a shiny crosshatch of thick white icing, a scattering of flaked almonds and some fresh raspberries to finish this classic bake.

Serves 12

75g unsalted butter, softened
50g caster sugar
1 medium egg
75g ground almonds
75g icing sugar
2 teaspoons toasted flaked almonds
25g raspberries

For the jam
75g raspberries
25g granulated sugar

For the pastry
125g plain flour
25g icing sugar
75g unsalted butter, softened
1 medium egg yolk

You will need
18cm round cake tin
baking paper
small piping bag

Lightly grease the cake tin with a little butter and line with a circle of baking paper.

To make the jam, put the 75g raspberries and granulated sugar in a saucepan with 2 tablespoons of water. Put over a medium heat for around 5 minutes, stirring occasionally to prevent burning and to help break down the raspberries. Keep the mixture simmering until you have a thick syrup, then remove the pan from the heat and pour into a small bowl. Set aside.

To make the pastry, put the flour and icing sugar in a large bowl with the butter and use your fingers to rub together to a breadcrumb-like consistency. Add the egg yolk and bring the pastry together into a smooth, soft dough. Turn out onto a clean surface and use your hands to knead the dough for 30 seconds or until all the egg yolk has been incorporated. Wrap the dough in cling film and chill in the fridge for 15 minutes.

Lay a sheet of baking paper onto a clean work surface. Remove the cling film from the dough and put the dough on the baking sheet. Roll out to 3–5mm thick and slightly larger than the tin you are using. Don't worry if your pastry sticks or tears a little; keep rolling gently until it comes back together.

Gently lift the paper and flip the pastry into the prepared tin, then discard the paper. Gently press the pastry onto the base and edges of the tin. Cut off the excess pastry, leaving a 1cm overhang around the edge. Prick the base of the tart all over with a fork, then spread the jam evenly into the bottom of the pastry case and put the tin into the fridge for at least 15 minutes to chill while you make the filling.

Preheat the oven to 180°C/160°C fan/gas mark 4. In a large bowl, beat the butter and sugar together with a wooden spoon until light and fluffy. Add the egg and mix again. Finally add the ground almonds and stir until combined (don't over mix).

Remove the tin from the fridge and spoon in the filling, smoothing it over the jam layer until level. Try to avoid swirling the jam into the filling.

Bake the tart in the oven for 20–30 minutes until lightly golden all over. A skewer inserted into the centre should come out clean. Remove from the oven and leave in the tin on a wire rack to cool completely. You may wish to trim your pastry further by running a small sharp knife around the edge of the tin. Once cooled, gently remove the tart from the tin, discard the baking paper and position onto the centre of a plate ready to decorate.

Put the icing sugar in a bowl and stir in 2–3 teaspoons of water. You need to do this gradually as you want a thick, glue-like icing for your tart. Put the icing into the piping bag and snip 0.5cm off the end. Start by piping around the edge of the tart to create a 1–2cm border, then pipe a crosshatch pattern on top. Decorate the iced edges of the tart with flaked almonds and finish with the raspberries.

BAKING TRAY RECIPES

CARAMEL YULE LOG

Start the festive season off on the right foot with this tempting caramel Yule log. A light chocolate Swiss roll filled with an oozy caramel sauce and fluffy whipped cream. The Yule log is topped with a rich chocolate frosting, a sprinkling of chopped hazelnuts and a snowy dusting of icing sugar.

Serves 10

4 medium eggs, separated
75g icing sugar
75g self-raising flour
2 tablespoons cocoa
   powder
½ teaspoon vanilla extract
2 tablespoons caster sugar
250ml double cream
15g hazelnuts, roughly
   chopped
10g icing sugar

For the caramel
50g caster sugar
pinch of salt
50ml double cream

For the icing
125g dark chocolate
125ml double cream

You will need
baking tray, approx.
   30 x 20 x 2cm
baking paper

Preheat the oven to 180°C/160°C fan/gas mark 4. Line the baking tray with a sheet of baking paper.

Whisk the egg whites in a bowl until they form stiff peaks. Gradually whisk in the icing sugar, then add the egg yolks one at a time and continue whisking until the mixture is really pale and light.

Fold in the flour, cocoa powder and vanilla extract. Ensure the mixture is fully combined, but be careful you don't over mix.

Spoon the mixture into the lined tray, then gently and evenly spread it to the edges of the tin and give the tray a few sharp taps on a flat surface to disperse any air bubbles. Bake for 8–10 minutes, or until it is cooked through evenly and springy to touch.

Put a second sheet of baking paper on a flat surface and sprinkle the caster sugar over it evenly. While the sponge is still warm and flexible, turn it out, top down, onto the sugared paper. Peel off the first sheet of baking paper and discard. Leave to cool.

For the caramel filling, combine the sugar and salt with 50ml of water in a saucepan. Stir over a medium heat until the sugar has dissolved, then simmer for 5 minutes, continuing to stir until it becomes golden in colour. Watch this closely as it can easily burn. Remove the caramel from the heat and then immediately add the 50ml of double cream and stir well until it has all combined. If lumps form, just keep stirring – the caramel should be a creamy colour and quite runny. Transfer to a bowl and leave to cool completely at room temperature.

Whisk the 250ml of double cream in a bowl until stiff. To assemble the cake, spread the whipped cream over the top of the flat sponge, then drizzle the caramel sauce on top. Start to roll the sponge tightly from the shortest side inwards, using the baking paper to help with the rolling. Chill in the fridge for 15 minutes.

For the icing, put the dark chocolate in a heatproof bowl. Heat the cream in a pan until it just begins to boil, then pour it over the chocolate. Stir with a wooden spoon until the chocolate has melted and the icing is thick enough to spread. Cool in the fridge for 10–15 minutes.

When the rolled sponge and icing have cooled, remove both from the fridge and spread the icing over the cake, leaving the ends exposed. Lightly run a fork through the icing to create a log effect. Sprinkle the hazelnuts on top and finish by dusting lightly with icing sugar.

CARROT CAKE COOKIES

For a fun twist on a classic carrot cake, try baking this scrumptious batch of subtly spiced carrot, oat and raisin cookies, drizzled with a glossy cream cheese icing. Adjust the baking time to achieve the perfect level of gooeyness for you. These are the perfect picnic treat.

Makes 12–15

55g unsalted butter,
   melted and cooled
85g light brown soft sugar
50g caster sugar
1 large egg
100g grated carrot
140g plain flour
1 teaspoon baking powder
½ teaspoon salt
1 teaspoon ground
   cinnamon
140g oats
85g raisins

For the icing
30g full-fat cream cheese
1 tablespoon milk
140g icing sugar

You will need
2 baking trays
baking paper
small piping bag

Preheat the oven to 180°C/160°C fan/gas mark 4. Line the baking trays with baking paper. If you only have one tray, you may need to bake in two batches, using a fresh sheet of baking paper for each batch.

In a large bowl, mix together the melted butter and the sugars until smooth. Add the egg and beat until well combined, then stir in the grated carrot until it is coated in the mixture and well distributed.

Gradually add the flour, baking powder, salt and cinnamon, stirring after each addition. Mix in the oats and raisins.

For each cookie, you will need roughly 2 tablespoons of mixture. Position each one on the baking tray, spacing them at least 5cm apart, as they will spread during cooking, then flatten slightly with the back of a spoon. You should have enough mixture to make 12–15 cookies.

Bake for 15–20 minutes, depending on how gooey you like your cookies. They should be slightly golden around the edges.

Remove from the oven and allow to cool and harden on the baking tray for 10 minutes before transferring to a wire rack to cool completely.

To make the icing, combine the cream cheese, milk and icing sugar in a bowl. Spoon the icing into the piping bag and snip a small piece off the end. Pipe the icing over your cookies and allow to set before serving.

TOP TIP
As an alternative to cream cheese, use 30g unsalted butter in the icing.

CARROT CAKE WHOOPIE PIES

Delicately spiced, crunchy carrot cake cookies sandwiched together with a subtle cinnamon buttercream. The whoopie pies are decorated with a sweet drizzle of white chocolate and a colourful sprinkle of crushed pistachios. Enjoy this generous batch during your coffee break (or any time you happen to pass the kitchen).

Makes 24

115g unsalted butter,
  melted and cooled
90g soft light brown sugar
80g caster sugar
½ teaspoon vanilla extract
1 medium egg, plus
  1 medium egg yolk
150g finely grated carrot
  (about 2–3 large carrots)
190g plain flour
1¼ teaspoons ground
  cinnamon
¾ teaspoon baking powder
½ teaspoon ground ginger
40g white chocolate
5g pistachios, crushed

For the buttercream

100g unsalted butter,
  softened
200g icing sugar
¼ teaspoon ground
  cinnamon

You will need

2–4 baking trays
baking paper
2 large piping bags

Preheat the oven to 180°C/160°C fan/gas mark 4. Grease the baking trays with a little butter and line with baking paper. If you have fewer than four trays, you will need to bake in batches, using a fresh sheet of baking paper for each batch.

In a large bowl, combine the melted butter, sugars and vanilla extract. Add the egg and egg yolk and mix until fully incorporated.

Put the grated carrot into a sieve and press most of the moisture out using the back of a spoon. The total drained weight should be around 125g. Fold the carrots into the mixture until they are completely coated.

Add the flour, cinnamon, baking powder and ginger and mix until fully combined.

Spoon the mixture into a piping bag and cut 3cm off the end. Pipe flat rounds of mixture, no higher than 1cm and about the size of a 50p piece, onto the prepared baking trays. Leave a 3–4cm gap between each cookie, as they will spread during cooking. Pipe 48 cookies, in as many batches as you need to.

Bake for 12 minutes, then check the cookies. If the tops are set and the edges are golden, remove from the oven; otherwise, bake for an additional 3–8 minutes, as needed. Leave to cool on the baking tray for 5 minutes, then transfer to a wire rack to cool completely.

While the cookies are cooling, make the buttercream. Beat the butter in a bowl and gradually add the icing sugar and cinnamon. Beat until thick and combined. If the buttercream is too firm to pipe, loosen it with a teaspoon of water.

To assemble the whoopie pies, spoon the buttercream into the second piping bag and cut 3cm off the end. Once the biscuits have cooled completely, turn half of them upside-down. Pipe a drop of buttercream into the middle of each of the upside-down biscuits, then sandwich the remaining biscuits on top, pressing them together.

Break the white chocolate into a heatproof bowl positioned over a pan of simmering water, making sure the bowl does not touch the water. Stir the chocolate until melted. Carefully remove the bowl from the saucepan and leave to cool slightly, then drizzle over the whoopie pies using a spoon. Before the drizzle sets, sprinkle the crushed pistachios over the very centre of the pies.

ALMOND & APRICOT BISCOTTI

A toasted almond, apricot and lemon zest biscuit, baked until crisp
and drizzled with white chocolate. This makes a batch of sweet
Italian biscuits, perfect for dipping in a piping hot coffee.

Makes 24

45g almonds, roughly
  chopped
60g unsalted butter,
  melted and cooled
170g caster sugar
2 eggs
zest of ½ lemon
240g plain flour
30g ground almonds
1½ teaspoons baking
  powder
60g dried apricots,
  chopped
40g white chocolate

You will need
2 baking trays
baking paper
small piping bag

Preheat the oven to 180°C/160°C fan/gas mark 4 and line the baking trays with
baking paper. If you only have one tray, you will need to bake in two batches,
using a fresh sheet of baking paper for each batch.

Lightly toast the chopped almonds in a frying pan. They are done when the nuts turn
golden brown and release a nutty aroma. Set aside to cool.

Beat the melted butter and sugar together in a bowl until combined. Add the eggs, one
at a time, beating well after each addition. Add the lemon zest and up to 1 tablespoon
of water (if needed) and stir through.

Add the flour, ground almonds and baking powder and mix gently until you have
a thick batter. Mix the apricots and toasted almonds into the batter until evenly
distributed throughout.

Spoon the batter into two equal long rows (one on each prepared baking tray), and
use the back of a spoon to flatten each one to around 25 x 8cm.

Bake for 20–25 minutes, or until the biscotti turn a light golden brown. Remove from
the oven and reduce the temperature to 130°C/110°C fan/gas mark 1. Leave to cool
for 10 minutes.

Move each biscotti onto a chopping board and, using a sharp knife, slice into
2cm-thick pieces. For a longer, more elegant biscuit, cut your biscotti at an angle.
Put each piece back onto the baking tray on its side. Return to the oven for 15–20
minutes, turning halfway through, until crunchy on both sides. When ready, transfer
the biscotti to a wire rack to cool.

Break the white chocolate into a heatproof bowl and position over a pan of simmering
water, making sure the bowl does not touch the water. Allow to melt. Spoon the melted
chocolate into the piping bag, snip off a small corner and drizzle the chocolate over the
cooled biscuits. Allow to set before serving.

CHOCOLATE & HAZELNUT WREATH

A luxurious chocolatey braided wreath studded with gleaming cranberries and scattered with crunchy fragments of toasted hazelnut. This delicious wreath makes an eye-catching centrepiece for your Christmas table, or a sensational festive breakfast for the whole family. Why not enjoy this bake slightly warm from the oven?

Serves 12–15

45g unsalted butter, softened
250g strong white bread flour
13g caster sugar
½ teaspoon fine salt
150ml lukewarm milk
3.7g quick yeast
30g dried cranberries
1 egg yolk
1 teaspoon milk
15g blanched hazelnuts, chopped
1 teaspoon icing sugar

For the chocolate spread

45g dark chocolate
50g unsalted butter
75g soft light brown sugar
1 tablespoon cocoa powder
20g dark chocolate chips

You will need

large baking tray
baking paper

Put the butter in a bowl with the flour, sugar and salt and rub together with your fingers until you have a fine breadcrumb-like mixture. Add the milk and yeast and mix with a wooden spoon to form a dough, bringing it together by hand. Knead the dough on a clean surface for 5–10 minutes. The dough will be smooth and if you press it with your finger it will bounce back slightly. Transfer the dough to a clean bowl and cover with cling film, then leave to rise somewhere warm for 60–90 minutes, until doubled in size.

For the chocolate spread, break the dark chocolate into a heatproof bowl positioned over a pan of simmering water, making sure the bowl doesn't touch the water, and stir until the chocolate has melted. Set aside for a few minutes to cool slightly.

In a large bowl, combine the melted chocolate with the butter, light brown sugar, cocoa powder and dark chocolate chips. Mix everything together until you have a smooth, spreadable mixture, then set aside.

When the dough has risen, remove it from the bowl and put onto a sheet of baking paper. Roll out the dough into a rectangular shape, approx. 45 x 25cm. Spread the chocolate mixture gently and evenly across the dough, then scatter over half the dried cranberries.

With the long side facing you, tightly roll the dough so it resembles a long sausage shape, using the paper to help if necessary. Lift the dough onto a second piece of baking paper and put it onto the baking tray.

Use a sharp knife to gently cut the roll in half down its length, leaving one end intact. Twist the strips together, then shape into a circle and pinch the ends to make a wreath. Cover the baking tray loosely with cling film and leave the wreath to prove somewhere warm for 25–30 minutes.

Preheat the oven to 180°C/160°C fan/gas mark 4. In a small bowl, combine the egg yolk and milk to create an egg wash, then brush the egg wash over the proved wreath and sprinkle over the hazelnuts. Scatter the remaining cranberries on top.

Bake the wreath for 25–30 minutes until golden brown. Leave to cool for 10–15 minutes on the baking tray before carefully removing from the paper and placing onto a board or plate. Use a sieve to dust with the icing sugar and serve warm.

CUSTARD CREAM
BISCUITS

The delicately crunchy custardy dough, sandwiched together
with the smooth, thick custard buttercream, give these biscuits
a wonderful contrast in texture. This is a classic British biscuit
favourite and is best enjoyed, as any biscuit should be, with
a cup of tea. Just try not to eat the whole lot in one go…

Makes 22–30

225g unsalted butter,
  softened
115g caster sugar
3 tablespoons milk
340g plain flour
125g custard powder

For the filling
120g unsalted butter,
  softened
210g icing sugar
20g custard powder

You will need
2 baking trays
baking paper
small piping bag

Line the baking trays with baking paper. If you only have one tray, you will need
to bake in batches, using a fresh sheet of baking paper for each batch.

In a bowl, beat the butter with the sugar until light and fluffy.

Add the milk and beat into the mixture, then add the flour and custard powder
and mix together until you have a smooth dough. You'll need to bring the mixture
together with your hands.

Roll and shape the dough into a long rectangle, approx. 40 x 4cm, and 5cm thick.
Wrap in cling film and chill in the fridge for at least 2 hours until firm.

Once chilled, thinly slice the dough (it should make around 44–60 slices) and
transfer to the prepared baking trays; you can sit the biscuits closely together
as they don't spread much during cooking.

Preheat the oven to 180°C/160°C fan/gas mark 4. Using a skewer, decorate each
biscuit by dotting around the edge, keeping within 0.5cm of the edge.

Bake for 10–15 minutes, or until the edges of the biscuits turn a pale golden brown
colour. Remove from the oven and allow to cool for 5–10 minutes on the tray before
transferring the biscuits to a wire rack to cool completely.

For the filling, beat the butter in a bowl until really soft, then add the icing sugar and
custard powder and mix to combine. Gradually add 1–2 teaspoons of water and mix
until you have a smooth, thick buttercream.

Lay out half the biscuits upside-down on a clean work surface. Spoon the filling
into the piping bag, then snip about 2cm off the end and pipe the buttercream
onto the biscuit bases in a zig-zag formation, to the same thickness as the biscuits
themselves. Top with the remaining biscuits and, once assembled, chill the finished
biscuits for 20–30 minutes in the fridge to firm up the icing. These are best served
at room temperature.

WHOOPIE PIES

A tempting, generous batch of whoopie pies made from freshly baked rich chocolate cookies and sandwiched together with a thick white chocolate buttercream. Each whoopie pie is a convenient mouthful, and as they're so moreish, why stop at just the one?

Makes 24

110g unsalted butter, softened
50g caster sugar
100g soft light brown sugar
1 teaspoon vanilla extract
1 medium egg
260g plain flour
60g cocoa powder
¼ teaspoon bicarbonate of soda
¼ teaspoon baking powder
⅛ teaspoon salt
40ml milk

For the filling
75g white chocolate
110g icing sugar
75g unsalted butter, softened

You will need
2 baking trays
baking paper
large piping bag

In a large bowl, cream together the butter, sugars and vanilla. Then add the egg, flour, cocoa powder, bicarbonate of soda, baking powder and salt and mix well.

Add the milk and mix until it forms a firm and slightly sticky dough. If it becomes too stiff to mix with a spoon, work it with your hands until well combined.

Roll into a sausage shape around 30cm in length, cover with cling film and refrigerate for 20 minutes.

Preheat the oven to 180°C/160°C fan/gas mark 4. Line the baking trays with baking paper. If you only have one tray, you will need to bake in batches, using a fresh sheet of baking paper for each batch.

Once chilled, divide the dough into 48 equal pieces and roll into small balls. Put them on the lined baking tray(s) and bake for 8–10 minutes, or until set and the tops spring back when lightly touched. Allow to cool for 5 minutes on the tray before transferring to a wire rack to cool completely.

While the biscuits are cooling, prepare the filling. Break the white chocolate into a heatproof bowl and position over a pan of simmering water. Allow the chocolate to melt, making sure the bowl does not touch the water. In a separate bowl, combine the icing sugar with the butter. Add the melted chocolate and mix thoroughly with the buttercream until smooth but stiff. Chill in the fridge for 10 minutes if needed.

Spoon the buttercream filling into the piping bag and snip 2cm off the end of the bag. Once the biscuits have cooled completely, turn half of them upside-down. Pipe a drop of buttercream into the middle of each of the upside-down biscuits. Sandwich the remaining biscuits on top, pressing together gently, and enjoy!

TOP TIP
Pop half of the uncooked, unsliced dough into the freezer, wrapped in cling film, and freeze for up to 3 months. Allow to return to room temperature before baking as directed.

OAT & GINGER BISCUITS

A liberal batch of tempting oaty biscuits, generously studded with pieces of crystallised ginger, and coated in a textured mix of crunchy demerara sugar, oats and ginger. To finish, the biscuits are artistically drizzled with a rich melted dark chocolate. A robust biscuit to dunk in a nice cup of tea.

Makes 15–18

225g unsalted butter, softened
200g soft light brown sugar
1 large egg yolk
225g self-raising flour
⅛ teaspoon salt
1 teaspoon ground ginger
100g oats
50g crystallised ginger
50g dark chocolate chips

For the coating
25g oats
10g crystallised ginger
20g demerara sugar

You will need
2 baking trays
baking paper

Preheat the oven to 190°C/170°C fan/gas mark 5. Line the baking trays with baking paper. If you only have one tray, you will need to bake in two batches, using a fresh sheet of baking paper for each batch.

Beat the butter and light brown sugar in a bowl until light and fluffy, then mix in the egg yolk.

Add the flour, salt and ground ginger and combine to form a soft dough. Mix in the oats and the crystallised ginger.

Roll the dough into a sausage shape, wrap in cling film and refrigerate for 10 minutes. After 10 minutes, divide the dough into 15–18 balls.

For the coating, combine the oats, ginger and demerara sugar in a small bowl. Press the dough balls firmly into the oat mix, ensuring an even covering of each biscuit.

Transfer to the prepared baking tray(s), leaving some space between them as they will spread out during cooking.

Bake for 10 minutes, or until the biscuits begin to turn golden in colour. Allow to cool on the tray for 5 minutes, then transfer to a wire rack to cool completely.

Put the dark chocolate chips into a heatproof bowl positioned over a pan of simmering water, making sure the bowl does not touch the water. Heat until melted, then drizzle the chocolate generously over the biscuits. Allow the chocolate to harden, and enjoy! The biscuits will keep in an airtight container for a few days.

TOP TIP
Wrap half of the uncooked dough in cling film and freeze until you're ready for your next biscuit fix. Allow to return to room temperature before baking as above.

SOFT PRETZELS

Sixteen perfectly shaped pretzels, to either coat in cinnamon sugar or dip in a rich chocolate sauce (or both). They're particularly delicious served warm from the oven, so bake in batches when you are ready to eat them. These are such a versatile bake. Why not try coating them in garlic butter, or topping with some coarse salt?

Makes 16

115g unsalted butter
350ml milk
570g strong white bread
  flour, plus extra to dust
30g caster sugar
⅛ teaspoon salt
7g quick yeast
2 tablespoons bicarbonate
  of soda

For the cinnamon sugar
2 teaspoons ground
  cinnamon
65g caster sugar

For the chocolate
  dipping sauce
35ml milk
70g dark chocolate chips

You will need
2 baking trays
baking paper
slotted spoon

Melt 70g of butter in a small pan over a low heat and add the milk. Warm the mixture until it is just past lukewarm – if you have a thermometer, this is about 40°C; if not, it should be a comfortable temperature when tested with your finger. If it is too hot to keep your finger in for a few seconds, leave it to cool slightly. If the milk is too hot, it will prevent the dough from rising.

Put the flour in a large bowl. Add the sugar, salt and yeast and mix until well combined. Make a well in the flour mixture, then pour in the warmed milk and butter. Mix everything together with a wooden spoon until a soft dough forms.

Dust a clean work surface with flour and tip the dough onto it. Grease the inside of a large, clean bowl with a little butter and set aside. Knead the dough by stretching it away from you with the heel of one hand and folding it back over the top towards you. Continue to knead for 8–10 minutes until the dough is smooth and elastic.

Shape the dough into a ball and put it in the greased bowl. Cover with cling film or a tea towel and leave in a warm place for 60–90 minutes, or until the dough has doubled in size. Put the dough onto a clean surface and knead a couple of times to knock the air out. Position the dough on a chopping board and use a large knife to cut it into 16 equal pieces (cut the dough into quarters, then cut each quarter into four). Roll each piece into a long rope, approximately 50cm long.

To shape the pretzel, curve the rope of dough into an upside down 'U', then twist the ends together twice, by wrapping the left end over the right end each time. Bring the twisted ends up towards the top and press firmly onto the top curve of the pretzel to secure the ends. Repeat for all 16 pretzels.

Preheat the oven to 200°C/180°C fan/gas mark 6. Line the baking trays with baking paper. If you only have one tray, you will need to bake in two batches, using a fresh sheet of baking paper for each batch.

Fill a pan 10cm deep with water and bring to the boil. Carefully add the bicarbonate of soda and reduce to a simmer. Using a slotted spoon, put one pretzel at a time into the water. Soak each pretzel for 10 seconds per side, then remove with the slotted spoon, drain the water from the pretzel, and transfer each to the prepared baking tray(s). Once all are dipped, bake in the oven for 10–15 minutes until golden.

While the pretzels are baking, put the cinnamon and sugar into a medium-sized shallow bowl and ensure they are thoroughly combined. Melt the remaining butter in a pan. As soon as the pretzels come out of the oven, brush with the melted butter, then leave to cool for a couple of minutes. Leaving some pretzels plain (to dip in the chocolate sauce), toss the rest in the bowl of cinnamon sugar, coating the top and bottom of each pretzel.

To make the chocolate dipping sauce, warm the milk in a small saucepan until just below boiling. Put the dark chocolate chips in a heatproof bowl and pour the milk over the chocolate. Let it sit for 1 minute, then stir to combine until it is smooth and the chocolate has melted. The dipping sauce thickens as it cools, so make it just before you tuck in. The pretzels are best enjoyed warm from the oven.

CHOCOLATE ORANGE HOT CROSS BUNS

These hot cross buns are light, airy, full of flavour and extra delicious toasted and spread with lashings of butter. They're well worth the extra effort – you'll never buy ready-made buns again.

Makes 12

150ml milk
grated zest of 1 large
   orange
150g unsalted butter
10g quick yeast
470g strong white bread
   flour, plus extra to dust
50g soft light brown sugar
1 teaspoon ground
   mixed spice
1 tcaspoon ground
   cinnamon
½ teaspoon salt
1 large egg
100g dark chocolate chips

For the glaze
1 tablespoon orange juice
20g orange marmalade
10g caster sugar

You will need
2 baking trays
baking paper
piping bag

Put the milk and 20ml of water in a pan over a low heat and bring to a simmer, then take it off the heat. Stir in the orange zest and butter until melted, then leave to cool until just warmer than room temperature. Add the yeast and stir through.

Combine 400g flour with the sugar, spices and salt in a large bowl, making sure there are no lumps of sugar. Pour in the warm milk mixture, then add the egg. Starting with a wooden spoon, gently bring all of the ingredients together until a dough forms, bringing it together with your hands if needed.

Lightly flour a work surface and tip the dough onto it. Knead the dough for 10 minutes, until it is a springy and smooth ball. Put the dough into a clean bowl, cover with cling film and leave in a warm place to rise for 2 hours or until it has doubled in size.

Add the dark chocolate chips to the dough and knead until they are distributed throughout.

Line the baking trays with baking paper. If you only have one tray, you will need to bake in two batches, using a fresh sheet of baking paper for each batch. Divide the dough into 12 equal pieces and shape them into balls, trying to encase the chocolate. Tuck the edges of each bun underneath, pinching them together to make sure you have a smooth top. Put the buns on the lined tray(s) about 2cm apart. Cover with oiled cling film and leave them to prove in a warm place for 1–2 hours, until they have doubled in size and touching each other.

Preheat the oven to 190°C/170° fan/gas mark 5. Mix 4–5 tablespoons of water with the remaining flour until you have a very thick paste. Transfer to the piping bag and snip off the end. Pipe a continuous line of paste across each row and column of buns, then bake for 20 minutes or until golden brown.

For the glaze, combine the orange juice, marmalade and sugar in a small pan and heat gently until melted. Brush over the top of the warm buns and leave to cool before tearing apart to enjoy.

TOP TIPS

If you want freshly made buns for the morning, pop the buns in the fridge after the second prove and leave overnight. In the morning, let the buns rise for 1 hour before baking as directed.

To make traditional hot cross buns, reserve 1 tablespoon of orange juice for the glaze, and soak 100g sultanas in the remaining juice of one orange while you prepare the dough. Drain any juice from the sultanas and dry them with kitchen paper. Instead of the chocolate chips, add the sultanas to the dough, adding a little more flour if the dough is too wet. Shape the dough and bake as above for delicious hot cross buns.

ICED BUNS

Another British classic: the iced bun. A dozen delightfully fluffy, zesty bread rolls packed with mixed fruit and generously smothered with a glossy white icing. To complement the slight hint of lemon in the dough, why not add a squeeze of lemon to the icing for an added hit of flavour? Yum!

Makes 12

100g unsalted butter, softened
50g caster sugar
500g strong white bread flour, plus extra to dust
5g salt
7g quick yeast
1½ tablespoons lemon zest
1 egg
150ml lukewarm milk
50ml lukewarm water
70g mixed dried fruit (optional)
250g icing sugar
squeeze of lemon juice (optional)

You will need
baking tray
baking paper

In a large bowl, mix together the butter and sugar. Add the flour and salt and rub together with your fingers until the mixture resembles soft breadcrumbs. Add the yeast and lemon zest.

In a separate bowl, lightly beat the egg and milk together and pour into the butter and sugar mixture. Gradually add the lukewarm water, mixing until you get a slightly sticky and soft dough.

Dust a work surface with flour and knead the dough for 5 minutes, until soft and smooth. Put the dough into a clean bowl, cover and leave to rise in a warm place for 1–2 hours, or until the dough has doubled in size.

Once the dough has risen, sprinkle over the dried fruit, if using, and knead for a further minute or two. If not using the dried fruit, simply knead the dough briefly for a minute.

Shape into 12 equal-sized smooth balls, then roll these in your hands to make finger-shaped buns.

Line a baking tray with baking paper then place the buns on the tray in two lines of six, spacing them about 2cm apart. Put a lightly oiled piece of cling film over the buns and leave them somewhere warm to prove until they have doubled in size, about 30–60 minutes.

Preheat the oven to 200°C/180°C fan/gas mark 6. Bake the buns for 10–15 minutes, or until the tops are lightly golden (making sure they don't get too dark). Allow to cool completely.

In a bowl, combine the icing sugar with 2 tablespoons of water, gently mixing until you have a very thick icing. Alternatively, use a squeeze of fresh lemon juice in place of the water. Spread the icing generously over the tops of the buns and wait for it to harden slightly before serving.

CHOCOLATE & CARAMEL ECLAIRS

A totally irresistible batch of light, airy choux buns, filled with a sweetened whipped cream, topped with a choice of milk chocolate or caramel sauce and drizzled with white chocolate to give an elegant finish. An impressive addition to any afternoon tea, or a luxurious treat whenever you fancy.

Makes 12 (or 24 mini eclairs)

100g unsalted butter
5g caster sugar
3g salt
120ml milk, plus 1 extra tablespoon
150g plain flour
4 medium eggs, plus 1 medium egg yolk
50g white chocolate

For the chocolate icing
100g milk chocolate
60ml double cream

For the caramel icing
200g caster sugar
¼ teaspoon vanilla extract
60g unsalted butter
120ml double cream

For the cream filling
360ml double cream
20g icing sugar

You will need
1 large baking tray or 2 smaller baking trays
baking paper
2 piping bags

Put the butter, sugar, salt, 120ml of milk and 120ml of water into a large saucepan and warm over a low heat until the butter is melted. Turn up the heat and allow the mixture to come to the boil, then immediately remove the pan from the heat and add the flour – quickly and all in one go. Mix thoroughly with a wooden spoon until completely smooth. Return the pan to a medium heat and stir for about 1 minute to slightly dry out the mixture. Then remove from the heat and transfer the mixture to a bowl.

Add the 4 whole eggs, one at a time, beating with a wooden spoon all the time until the pastry is smooth and silky.

Preheat the oven to 200°C/180°C fan/ gas mark 6 and line the baking tray(s) with baking paper.

While the raw choux pastry is still warm, fill a piping bag with the mixture and cut 2cm off the end of the bag. For mini eclairs, pipe 24 eclairs around 6cm long onto the baking tray(s). For large eclairs, pipe 12 eclairs around 10cm long. Shape the ends so that they are slightly rounded; you can tidy them up using the back of a teaspoon dipped in hot water. Space them well apart as they increase in size as they bake.

Make the egg wash by beating the egg yolk with the tablespoon of milk. Brush the egg wash over the eclairs and bake for 20–25 minutes, until crisp and golden brown on the outside. Transfer to a wire rack to cool, and prick each one in the side with a skewer to allow the steam to escape.

For the chocolate icing, put the milk chocolate and cream in a pan over a gentle heat. When the chocolate is melted, transfer it to a bowl and pop in the fridge to cool for 15 minutes.

For the caramel icing, put the caster sugar and vanilla extract in a pan over a low heat, stirring continuously until the sugar is smooth and light brown. Remove from the heat, add the butter then slowly add the double cream, continuing to stir until the sauce thickens.

For the cream filling, whip the double cream to soft peaks and gently fold in the icing sugar. Fill a piping bag with the cream, snip off the end, and, when the eclairs are cool, cut a small slit in the side of each one and pipe some cream in. Spread the chocolate and caramel toppings over the eclairs and allow to set.

Melt the white chocolate in a bowl positioned over a pan of simmering water, making sure the bowl doesn't touch the water. Leave to cool slightly, then drizzle the melted chocolate over the tops of the eclairs.

TOP TIP
Measure out all the ingredients before you start – everything happens quite quickly and it helps to be prepared.

SQUARE TIN RECIPES

BLUEBERRY & CASHEW SQUARES

A light, buttery dough base layered with gooey blueberry jam and a scattering of crumbled dough. These squares are topped with smooth fragments of toasted cashew nuts and crunchy demerara sugar. Deliciously tempting, these squares would make a delightful weekend breakfast or a wonderful mid-morning snack any day of the week.

Serves 12–16

315g plain flour
1 teaspoon baking powder
¼ teaspoon salt
180g unsalted butter, cold, diced
240g granulated sugar
1 medium egg
4 tablespoons cornflour
200g blueberries
20g cashew nuts, roughly chopped
1 tablespoon demerara sugar

You will need
20cm square baking tin
baking paper

Preheat the oven to 190°C/170°C fan/gas mark 5. Grease the tin with a little butter and line with a sheet of baking paper. Lightly grease this paper and lay another sheet the opposite way on top to cover all four sides.

Put the plain flour, baking powder and salt in a medium bowl with the butter and use your fingers to rub everything together until the mixture resembles breadcrumbs.

Stir in 160g granulated sugar and the egg and use a wooden spoon to bring the mixture together into a crumbly dough.

Spoon half the dough into the prepared tin, using your fingers to press it evenly into the base of the tin.

In a separate bowl, put the remaining granulated sugar, cornflour and blueberries along with 2 tablespoons of water. Mix everything together, then tip the blueberry mixture into the tin on top of the dough.

Now add the remaining dough on top of the blueberry layer. The dough might be a little sticky, so use your fingers to pull it apart and arrange it on top, leaving some blueberries on show. Once baked, this will form a crumble topping. Sprinkle the chopped cashew nuts and demerara sugar over the top.

Bake for 40–50 minutes, until the top is golden brown. Leave to cool in the tin on a wire rack, then remove from the tin and cut into 12–16 pieces.

TOP TIP
The squares are a perfect teatime treat. Alternatively, they can be enjoyed as a dessert with the addition of cream or crème anglaise.

CHERRY CRUMBLE SQUARES

Light, chewy squares stuffed with deliciously sweet glacé cherries and topped with a crunchy cinnamon crumble. These sticky, yummy little squares will get your taste buds tingling. Try serving them warm with an extra dollop of sour cream for a truly delicious dessert.

Serves 12–16

65g unsalted butter,
  softened
130g soft light brown sugar
80ml sour cream
2 eggs, beaten
130g self-raising flour
225g glacé cherries,
  halved
20g icing sugar

For the crumble mix
100g self-raising flour
1 teaspoon ground
  cinnamon
50g unsalted butter
50g demerara sugar

You will need
20cm square baking tin
baking paper

Preheat the oven to 180°C/160°C fan/gas mark 4. Lightly grease the tin with a little butter and line with a sheet of baking paper.

In a large bowl, cream together the butter and light brown sugar until light and fluffy. Add the sour cream and eggs and mix in, then gently fold in the flour until just combined.

Pour the batter into the prepared tin. Position the halved cherries evenly over the top and bake for 10 minutes.

While the cake is baking, make the crumble mix. Put the flour, cinnamon and butter in a bowl and use your fingers to rub together until you have a slightly sticky breadcrumb texture. Stir through the demerara sugar.

After the cake has been in the oven for 10 minutes, sprinkle the prepared crumble mix evenly over the top. Return to the oven and bake for a further 30 minutes, or until a skewer inserted into the centre comes out clean. Allow to cool for 5 minutes in the tin before turning out onto a wire rack to cool completely.

Shortly before serving, cut into 12–16 squares, then use a sieve to lightly dust the icing sugar over the top.

CARROT & PECAN SQUARES

A mouth-wateringly spiced pecan and carrot cake topped with peaks of buttery cinnamon icing and crunchy, nutty shards of pecan brittle. This is an unusual take on a classic carrot cake, and once you've tried it, you might never go back. Just the thing to enjoy along with your morning coffee.

Serves 12–16

75g caster sugar
75g soft dark brown sugar
200ml vegetable oil
2 medium eggs
200g plain flour
1 teaspoon bicarbonate
  of soda
1 teaspoon baking powder
1 teaspoon ground
  cinnamon
½ teaspoon ground ginger
½ teaspoon salt
200g carrots (peeled
  weight), grated
25g pecan nuts, roughly
  chopped

For the pecan brittle
15g pecan nuts, roughly
  chopped
50g granulated sugar

For the buttercream
150g unsalted butter,
  at room temperature
180g icing sugar
1 teaspoon ground
  cinnamon
1 tablespoon milk

Preheat the oven to 180°C/160°C fan/gas mark 4. Grease the tin with a little butter and line with a sheet of baking paper. Lightly grease this paper and lay another sheet the opposite way on top to cover all four sides.

In a large bowl, whisk together the sugars, oil and eggs until smooth. Gradually beat in the flour, bicarbonate of soda, baking powder, cinnamon, ginger and salt until thoroughly mixed. Add the grated carrot and pecan nuts to the mixture and stir everything together.

Pour into the lined tin and bake for 35–45 minutes, until a skewer inserted into the centre of the cake comes out clean. Allow the sponge to cool in the tin for 20 minutes, then turn out onto a wire rack to cool completely.

While the cake is cooling, make the pecan brittle. Line a baking sheet with baking paper and arrange the chopped pecans closely together (in a shape about the size of your hand).

Put the sugar in a pan along with 1 tablespoon of water. Stir to combine, then simmer over a medium heat, trying not to stir again until the sugar reaches an amber colour, which should take 3–5 minutes. Be careful to keep an eye on the caramel, as it can burn if left too long on the heat. Remove from the heat, give it a stir, then carefully and slowly pour evenly over the pecans, making sure they are all covered. Leave to set completely.

When your cake and brittle have cooled, make the buttercream. Beat the butter in a bowl to soften, then add the icing sugar, cinnamon and milk and beat again until light and fluffy. You may wish to add another teaspoon or two of milk to make your buttercream really soft.

Spoon the buttercream into the piping bag and cut around 2cm off the end. Pipe small peaks of buttercream all over the top of your cake. Chop the cooled pecan

You will need
20cm square baking tin
baking paper
large piping bag

brittle finely and sprinkle over the buttercream. Finally, slice your cake into 12–16 pieces. This cake is best served at room temperature.

TOP TIP
For the perfect texture and an even bake, grate the carrot as finely as possible.

RASPBERRY & COCONUT SQUARES

An aromatic almond base layered with fresh raspberries and a coconut-flavoured crumb. After baking, the cake is topped with more fresh raspberries and some crunchy demerara sugar and baked again. The cake is finished with a delicate sprinkling of white chocolate curls. A perfectly sweet and fruity combination of tastes and textures.

Serves 12–16

250g self-raising flour
50g ground almonds
280g caster sugar
200g unsalted butter, diced
50g desiccated coconut
2 medium eggs, beaten
250g raspberries
15g demerara sugar
1 tablespoon white chocolate curls

You will need
20cm square baking tin
baking paper

Preheat the oven to 180°C/160°C fan/gas mark 4. Grease the tin with a little butter and line with a sheet of baking paper.

Put the flour in a large bowl with the ground almonds and sugar. Add the butter and rub the mixture together between your fingers until well combined – it may be a little lumpy, but that is fine.

Transfer 85g of the mixture to a medium-sized bowl, stir the coconut into this bowl and set aside.

Add the eggs to the mixture in the first bowl and mix with a wooden spoon until combined. It does not need to be very smooth. Spread this mixture into the prepared tin to create a base layer, then sprinkle half the raspberries over the top. Scatter the coconut mixture on top and bake for 45 minutes.

Remove the cake from the oven, dot the remaining raspberries over the surface then sprinkle over the demerara sugar and bake for a further 15 minutes, until the cake is firm. Test with a skewer – if it comes out almost clean, the cake is done.

Leave to cool in the tin for 15 minutes, then transfer to a wire rack to cool completely. Scatter over the white chocolate curls and cut into 12–16 pieces.

TOP TIP
These squares are delicious warm with a generous dollop of mascarpone or ice cream alongside.

CHOCOLATE & PECAN MILLIONAIRE SQUARES

A subtle take on a classic bake. These moreish millionaire squares consist of a delicate almond-scented shortbread topped with a gooey layer of thick pecan-studded caramel and a fine layer of dark chocolate. This bake cuts beautifully to give 16 perfect squares of deliciousness.

Serves 12–16

135g unsalted butter, softened
180g plain flour
55g soft light brown sugar
pinch of salt
20g ground almonds

For the caramel
50g unsalted butter
110g demerara sugar
pinch of salt
110ml double cream
30g roasted pecan nuts, roughly chopped

For the chocolate
35g unsalted butter
90g dark chocolate chips

You will need
20cm square baking tin
baking paper

Grease the tin with a little butter and line with a sheet of baking paper.

In a large bowl, briefly beat the butter until soft, then gradually add the flour, sugar and salt. Mix in the ground almonds until a soft dough forms.

Put the dough into the prepared tin and distribute with your fingers at first, then press and smooth the dough with the back of a spoon or a small palette knife.

Preheat the oven to 180°C/160°C fan/gas mark 4. Bake the shortbread for 25–30 minutes, or until lightly golden. Remove from the oven and transfer the tin to a wire rack. While still slightly warm, if the shortbread base has receded from the sides of tin, gently use the back of a spoon to push it to the edges. Leave to cool completely in the tin.

When the shortbread has cooled, begin to make the caramel. Put the butter, demerara sugar and salt in a saucepan over a low heat. Let the butter melt slightly, then add the double cream and stir continuously (be careful as the sauce will be hot). When everything is combined and the sugar has dissolved, turn the heat up slightly, continuing to stir. Let the sauce bubble for 1 minute, or until it has thickened, then remove from the heat and stir for a few seconds. Add the chopped pecans to the caramel and mix well.

Pour the caramel over the cooled shortbread and spread it to the corners using a spoon or small palette knife. Chill in the fridge for at least 1 hour to set fully.

For the chocolate layer, over a medium heat, stir together the butter and dark chocolate chips in a saucepan until melted. Pour the chocolate topping over the cooled caramel and spread to the edges to create a smooth, thin layer. Use a fork to make a wavy pattern in the chocolate.

Chill in the fridge for 2–3 hours until the chocolate topping has completely set. Remove from the fridge and rest for 5 minutes before cutting. Use a knife to loosen the bake from the sides of the tin and then cut into 12–16 pieces. Store in an airtight container in the fridge then allow the squares to come back to room temperature before serving.

TOP TIP
For a clean cut, run a sharp knife under hot water and wipe clean before cutting each slice.

STRAWBERRY & ALMOND SQUARES

A simple yet enticing summer bake made by marbling an almond-studded batter together with a sticky, thick strawberry compote topping, and with toasted, flaked almonds. These are absolutely yummy as they are and even more so when served warm with a big dollop of cream.

Serves 12–16

175g unsalted butter
275g soft light brown sugar
2 large eggs
200g plain flour
5g baking powder
50g almonds, roughly
   chopped
10g roasted flaked
   almonds, to decorate

For the strawberry
   compote
200g strawberries
35g granulated sugar

You will need
20cm square baking tin
baking paper

Start by making the strawberry compote. Remove the stalks from 160g of the strawberries and chop into roughly 2cm slices, then put them in a saucepan with the sugar and 1½ tablespoons of water. Bring to the boil, then simmer over a medium heat, uncovered, for 12–15 minutes. Stir occasionally, until the strawberries have broken down into a thick, jam-like consistency.

Remove the stalks and chop the remaining strawberries into 1cm slices, then stir into the compote and simmer for a further 2 minutes. Transfer the compote to a bowl and set aside to cool.

Preheat the oven to 180°C/160°C fan/gas mark 4. Grease the tin with a little butter and line with a sheet of baking paper.

Melt the butter in a saucepan over a medium heat, then remove from the heat and beat in the light brown sugar until smooth and combined. Transfer to a medium-sized bowl and leave to cool for 10–15 minutes.

Beat the eggs into the cooled butter mixture, then fold in the flour and baking powder until just combined. Stir through the chopped almonds.

Spread the mixture over the base of the prepared tin. Spoon the compote onto the mixture and use a skewer to create a swirl pattern effect.

Bake for 40–50 minutes. Check at 40 minutes by inserting a skewer into the centre – it should come out almost clean. The top should look shiny and slightly cracked, and the bake should be firm enough that it doesn't wobble when you shake the tin.

Cool completely in the tin before removing and cutting into 12–16 pieces. Sprinkle the roasted flaked almonds over the top to decorate.

TOP TIP
Serve warm with a generous helping of double cream or crème fraîche.

ROCKY ROAD BROWNIES

An inspired mix of two sensational classic desserts. This bake is an irresistible, gooey chocolate brownie, topped with an oozy caramel sauce, soft chewy marshmallows and crushed chocolate malt balls. A sweet, chocolatey, satisfying piece of brownie heaven. Perfection!

Serves 12–16

200g unsalted butter, softened
280g caster sugar
75g self-raising flour
50g cocoa powder
75g dark chocolate chips
3 medium eggs, beaten
10g mini marshmallows
20g chocolate malt balls

For the caramel
100g caster sugar
60ml double cream
30g unsalted butter

You will need
20cm square baking tin
baking paper

Preheat the oven to 180°C/160°C fan/gas mark 4. Grease the tin with a little butter and line with a sheet of baking paper.

In a large bowl, cream the butter and sugar together until light and fluffy. Add the flour, cocoa powder, dark chocolate chips and eggs and mix until combined.

Pour the mixture into the prepared tin and spread out evenly over the base. Bake for 35–45 minutes – it's best not to overcook the brownie, and cooking time can vary considerably from oven to oven. To test, a skewer inserted into the centre should come out almost clean.

For the caramel, heat the sugar in a pan over a low heat, stirring continuously until the sugar is smooth and light brown. It will start to form clumps before melting. Remove from the heat and quickly stir in the double cream and butter, mixing well. Don't worry if a few lumps form, just keep stirring until smooth.

Drizzle some of the caramel over the brownie and sprinkle marshmallows over the top.

Bash the malt balls carefully with a rolling pin and sprinkle over the brownie. Drizzle a little more caramel over the top and cut into 12–16 pieces.

TOP TIP
Save any leftover caramel in an airtight container and use it to top your favourite ice cream, pancakes or desserts.

WHITE CHOCOLATE & CRANBERRY SQUARES

Beautifully light and fluffy white chocolate cake squares, packed with juicy cranberries and topped with a smooth, decadent buttercream. The bake is finished with a sprinkling of chopped pistachios.

Serves 12–16

60g white chocolate
140g unsalted butter, softened
140g caster sugar
2 medium eggs
160g self-raising flour
¾ teaspoon baking powder
60ml whole milk
60g cranberries
10g pistachios, roughly chopped

For the icing
70g white chocolate
70g unsalted butter, softened
95g icing sugar

You will need
20cm square baking tin
baking paper

Preheat the oven to 180°C/160°C fan/gas mark 4. Grease the tin with a little butter and line with a sheet of baking paper.

Break the white chocolate into a heatproof bowl positioned over a pan of simmering water, making sure the bowl does not touch the water. Once the chocolate has melted, carefully remove the bowl and set aside to cool.

In a large bowl, cream the butter and sugar together until light and fluffy. Add the eggs one at a time, beating continuously.

Add the flour, baking powder and milk, and combine until very smooth and creamy, then stir through the cooled melted chocolate. Gently fold in the cranberries until evenly distributed throughout the batter.

Pour into the prepared tin and bake for 30–35 minutes, until golden brown and a skewer inserted into the centre comes out clean. Allow to cool for 5 minutes in the tin before transferring to a wire rack to cool completely.

For the icing, break the white chocolate into a heatproof bowl positioned over a pan of simmering water, making sure the bowl does not touch the water. Once melted, set aside to cool slightly.

In a large bowl, combine the butter and icing sugar, then add the melted white chocolate and mix thoroughly with the buttercream.

Once the cake has completely cooled, spread the buttercream icing evenly over the top, sprinkle over the chopped pistachios and cut into 12–16 squares.

TOP TIP
As an alternative, gently fold the chopped pistachios into the cake mix with the cranberries for a crunch throughout.

CHOCOLATE CHEESECAKE BROWNIES

A delicious three-layered brownie recipe; a chocolate brownie base, a sweet cream cheese filling and a chocolatey topping. After setting in the fridge, these brownies are satisfyingly chewy, with a lovely mixture of sweetness and tanginess. Make sure you get to eat one, as they won't hang around for long.

Serves 12–16

100g unsalted butter, softened
140g caster sugar
40g self-raising flour
25g cocoa powder
2 medium eggs, beaten
40g dark chocolate chips

For the cheesecake mix
200g full-fat cream cheese
2 medium egg yolks
60g caster sugar

For the chocolate topping
25g unsalted butter
35ml milk
100g dark chocolate chips

You will need
20cm square baking tin
baking paper

Preheat the oven to 180°C/160°C fan/gas mark 4. Grease the tin with a little butter and line with a sheet of baking paper.

In a large bowl, cream the butter and sugar together until light and fluffy. Add the flour, cocoa powder and eggs and mix. Add the dark chocolate chips and mix again until everything is well combined.

Transfer the brownie mixture to the prepared tin and spread evenly over the base. Bake for 25 minutes, until it is set around the edges but still has a slight wobble in the centre. Remove from the oven (leave the oven on) and set the tin on a wire rack to cool for 10 minutes. Use the back of a spoon or a spatula to gently press down onto the brownie to flatten it in the tin, starting from the edges and moving towards the centre. Leave to cool for another 10–15 minutes.

In a clean bowl, beat together the cream cheese, egg yolks and sugar until the mixture is smooth. If the mixture looks a little lumpy, use a whisk or fork to beat it for another minute.

Pour the cheesecake mixture over your brownie base. Smooth to the edges with the back of a spoon and give the tin a few sharp taps on the work surface to flatten it. Return to the oven for 25 minutes, or until the cream cheese layer is set and slightly golden around the edges. Initially it will seem a little wobbly, but it will firm up as it cools at room temperature.

When the cream cheese layer is completely cool, start making the chocolate topping. Heat the butter and milk in a pan until the butter has melted. Take the pan off the heat, add the chocolate chips and stir until melted and smooth.

Pour the chocolate over the cooled cream cheese layer, making sure the top is completely covered with chocolate, but spreading very gently as you do not want to mix the chocolate with the cream cheese underneath. Give the tin another gentle tap, then leave to cool for at least 3–4 hours in the fridge before cutting.

Carefully remove the brownie from the tin – you may need to use a knife to help loosen the edges – and cut into 12–16 pieces.

TOP TIP
To ensure clean layers in each brownie square, wipe your knife clean each time you slice. This will prevent the chocolate running into the cheesecake layer.

LEMON & ALMOND SQUARES

A light and tangy bake with a buttery shortbread base and a zesty lemon curd topping, finished with a scattering of toasted almonds and a delicate dusting of icing sugar. These squares give a robust citrus kick and are a delightful way to brighten a dreary day.

Serves 12–16

125g unsalted butter, softened
125g caster sugar
pinch of salt
175g plain flour
40g ground almonds
1 tablespoon milk
15g toasted flaked almonds
5g icing sugar

For the lemon topping
grated zest and juice of 3 lemons
160g caster sugar
20g plain flour
3 medium eggs, plus 1 medium egg yolk

You will need
20cm square baking tin
baking paper

Preheat the oven to 180°C/160°C fan/gas mark 4. Grease the tin with a little butter and line with a sheet of baking paper. Lightly grease this paper and lay another sheet the opposite way on top to cover all four sides.

In a large bowl, beat together the butter, sugar and salt until light and fluffy. Add the flour, ground almonds and milk and mix everything together with a wooden spoon, then use your hands to bring the mixture together to form a dough.

Put the dough into the prepared tin, using your fingers to press it over the base and into the corners. Use the back of a spoon to level and smooth the dough. Bake for 25–35 minutes, until golden, then remove from the oven and put the tin on a wire rack to cool. Leave the oven on.

While your shortbread is cooling, make the lemon topping. Combine the lemon zest, sugar and flour in a bowl. In a separate bowl, whisk together the lemon juice, eggs and egg yolk. Strain the mixture through a sieve into the bowl of dry ingredients and whisk everything together to combine.

When the tin is cool to the touch, slowly pour the lemon mixture over the shortbread. Very carefully return the tin to the oven, ensuring you do not spill any lemon topping, and bake for 30 minutes.

Remove from the oven, scatter over the toasted flaked almonds and bake for a further 5–10 minutes, until the topping has set, with a slight wobble in the middle. Remove from the oven and leave the tin on a wire rack until completely cool.

Run a knife very gently around the baking paper in the tin and use the paper to help you lift the bake out. Cut into 12–16 pieces, then use a sieve to dust with the icing sugar.

TOP TIP
To make the lemons easier to juice, roll them under your hand a few times on a flat work surface.

LOAF TIN RECIPES

STICKY TOFFEE BANANA LOAF

If you've got some over ripe bananas hanging out in the fruit bowl, what better way to use them up than a banana loaf? Every baker should have their go-to banana recipe, and this is ours. This delicious sticky toffee banana loaf is topped with a gooey drizzle of toffee sauce, and a generous handful of crunchy pecans.

Serves 8–10

2 ripe bananas
60g unsalted butter, softened
140g caster sugar
140g soft light brown sugar
2 teaspoons vanilla extract
2 medium eggs, beaten
280g self-raising flour
½ teaspoon salt
½ teaspoon bicarbonate of soda
20g pecan halves

For the toffee sauce
20g unsalted butter
1 tablespoon milk
45g soft light brown sugar

You will need
900g/2lb loaf tin
baking paper

Preheat the oven to 190°C/170°C fan/gas mark 5. Grease the tin with a little butter and line with a sheet of baking paper.

Mash the bananas in a bowl until all large lumps are gone, then set aside.

In a large bowl, cream together the butter, sugars and vanilla until light and fluffy. Add the eggs and mashed banana and mix well, then stir in the flour, salt and bicarbonate of soda.

Pour the mixture into the prepared tin and bake for 50 minutes, or until a skewer inserted into the centre comes out clean. Leave to cool in the tin for 10 minutes, then turn out onto a wire rack to cool completely.

For the toffee sauce, melt the butter in a small saucepan. Add the milk and sugar, then bring to the boil and allow to simmer for a couple of minutes, stirring continuously to prevent it burning.

Sprinkle the pecans on top of the loaf, then drizzle the toffee sauce over the top, allowing it to run down the sides. Let the sauce cool slightly before serving.

TOP TIP
The riper the bananas, the better! Not only do they make the loaf taste great, they're also easier to mash.

CINNAMON & PECAN LOAF

A tasty, crunchy loaf made with a sour cream cake batter. The loaf is layered with toasted, chopped pecans coated in cinnamon and demerara sugar, and the flavours are gently marbled together. The loaf is generously drizzled with a thick, white icing. Slice and enjoy.

Serves 10

50g pecan nuts, coarsely chopped
120g unsalted butter, softened
120g caster sugar
2 large eggs
180ml sour cream
210g self-raising flour
⅛ teaspoon salt
65g demerara sugar
1 tablespoon ground cinnamon
75g icing sugar

You will need
900g/2lb loaf tin
baking paper

Preheat the oven to 180°C/160°C fan/gas mark 4. Grease the tin with a little butter and line with a sheet of baking paper.

Toast the chopped pecans in a frying pan over a medium heat for 4–5 minutes, being careful not to let them burn. Set aside.

In a large bowl, beat together the butter and caster sugar until light and fluffy. Add the eggs one at time, continuing to beat the mixture until well combined. Add the sour cream and mix in gently. Add the flour and salt to the mixture and gently combine – it's very important not to over mix at this stage.

In a separate bowl, combine the demerara sugar, cinnamon and toasted pecans.

Pour half the cake mixture into the prepared loaf tin. Sprinkle half the cinnamon and pecan mixture on top. Spoon in the remaining cake mixture and smooth the top. Add the remaining cinnamon mixture and swirl around with a knife. Swirl the mixture a little more than you think it needs. This will ensure a good marbling of the cinnamon mixture throughout the loaf.

Bake on the middle shelf of the oven for around 50 minutes. Check the centre of the loaf with a skewer at 40 minutes, then every 5 minutes until the skewer comes out clean. Allow to cool in the tin for 10 minutes, then remove from the tin and transfer to a wire rack to cool completely.

Put the icing sugar in a medium bowl and mix with 1 tablespoon of water. You want the icing to be thick but smooth enough to drizzle. Using a spoon, drizzle the icing over the top of the loaf.

CHOCOLATE & VANILLA MARBLE LOAF

Chocolate and vanilla batters are gently marbled together to make this impressive loaf cake. The loaf is abundantly topped with a glossy dark chocolate glaze and decoratively feathered with white chocolate. Enjoy the attractive swirl of chocolate and vanilla with each slice.

Serves 12

30g dark chocolate
140g unsalted butter, softened
135g caster sugar
45g soft light brown sugar
5 tablespoons milk
15g cocoa powder
3g coffee granules
195g self-raising flour
1 teaspoon baking powder
2 teaspoons vanilla extract
3 medium eggs, beaten

For the glaze/icing
40g dark chocolate
10g cocoa powder
15g icing sugar
20g unsalted butter, softened
3 tablespoons boiling water
30g white chocolate

You will need
900g/2lb loaf tin
baking paper
small piping bag

Preheat the oven to 170°C/150°C fan/gas mark 3. Grease the tin with a little butter and line with a sheet of baking paper.

Break the dark chocolate into a heatproof bowl positioned over a pan of simmering water, making sure the bowl does not touch the water. Once the chocolate has melted, carefully remove the bowl and set aside to cool.

In a large bowl, cream the butter with the sugars for around 3 minutes, until light and fluffy.

Heat 3 tablespoons of milk in a pan or in a microwave until very hot but not boiling. In a mug, combine the cocoa powder and coffee together with the warmed milk and mix until smooth. Set aside to cool.

Combine the flour, baking powder and vanilla in a bowl. In alternate batches, gently fold the dry ingredients and the beaten eggs into the creamed butter mixture until just combined. Divide the batter equally between two bowls, then transfer 3 heaped tablespoons of one of the mixtures into the other bowl so one of the bowls contains a little more mixture.

Put the melted dark chocolate into the bowl with slightly less mixture in it, along with the cocoa powder and coffee mixture. Add the remaining milk to the non-chocolate mixture. Mix each one just until you have two smooth cake batters.

Spoon alternate dollops of the chocolate and plain batter into the prepared loaf tin until all is used up. Drag a skewer through the mixture to create a marbled effect, ensuring the skewer touches the bottom and all sides of the tin. It's up to you how marbled you'd like it, but be careful not to over mix the batters.

Bake for 40–50 minutes, or until the cake has started to shrink away from the edges of the tin and a skewer inserted into the centre comes out clean. Allow to cool for 20 minutes before removing from the tin and placing on a wire rack to cool fully.

For the glaze, put the dark chocolate, cocoa powder, icing sugar, butter and boiling water in a bowl and mix until all the ingredients have melted into a pourable glaze. Pour the glaze over the cooled loaf, letting it run down the sides a little. If the glaze is a little too thin, let the mixture cool for a few minutes.

Break the white chocolate into a heatproof bowl positioned over a pan of simmering water, making sure the bowl does not touch the water. Once melted, pour it into the piping bag. Snip a small corner off the end of the piping bag and, soon after the glaze has been poured, pipe lines of white chocolate across the top of the loaf, around 2cm apart. Drag a skewer up and down the loaf in the opposite direction to the piped lines to create a feathered effect. Allow the glaze to set before serving.

STICKY TOFFEE GINGER LOAF

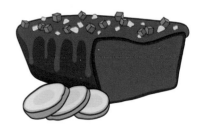

A rich date and ginger loaf draped with a smooth, sticky toffee sauce. The cake is abundantly scattered with pieces of chopped crystallised ginger and chewy fudge. The dates make the loaf beautifully fudgy, and the ginger adds a real warmth. A tempting autumnal bake, perhaps ideal for a Bonfire Night or Halloween party.

Serves 10

125g chopped dates
1 teaspoon bicarbonate
 of soda
180ml boiling water
60g unsalted butter
115g soft light brown sugar
2 medium eggs, beaten
145g self-raising flour
2 teaspoons ground ginger
15g crystallised ginger, cut
 into small cubes
20g mini fudge cubes

For the toffee sauce
25g unsalted butter
55g demerara sugar
55ml double cream

You will need
900g/2lb loaf tin
baking paper

Preheat the oven to 180°C/fan 160°C/gas mark 4. Grease the loaf tin with a little butter and line with a sheet of baking paper.

Put the chopped dates and bicarbonate of soda in a heatproof bowl with the boiling water, stir, and set aside to cool for 10 minutes.

Beat the butter and sugar together in a bowl until pale and fluffy. Add the beaten eggs together with the flour and ground ginger and mix until combined.

Add the date mixture to the bowl and stir together, then pour the mixture into the prepared loaf tin.

Bake on the lowest shelf of the oven for 15 minutes, then reduce the oven temperature to 170°C/150°C fan/gas mark 3 and cook for a further 30–40 minutes, until a skewer inserted into the centre comes out clean. Leave to cool in the tin for 20 minutes, then remove from the tin and leave to cool completely on a wire rack.

Meanwhile, for the toffee sauce put the butter and sugar in a saucepan over a low heat. Let the butter melt slightly, then add the double cream and stir continuously (be careful as the sauce will be hot). Once the ingredients have combined and the sugar has dissolved, increase the heat slightly, continuing to stir. Let the sauce bubble for 1 minute, until it has thickened, then take off the heat and stir for a few seconds before pouring into a heatproof jug or bowl. Set aside to cool.

When the sauce has cooled, give it a little stir, then pour over the loaf, letting it run down the edges. Scatter the crystallised ginger evenly over the toffee sauce, then sprinkle over the fudge cubes.

APPLE CRUMBLE & CUSTARD LOAF

A comforting, wintry apple loaf filled and topped with a delicate custard buttercream and scattered with a crunchy crumble topping, giving a lovely mix of tastes and textures. Enjoy the flavours of a classic apple crumble without the need for a spoon. The perfect way to brighten a cold winter's day.

Serves 10

95g unsalted butter, at
    room temperature
165g self-raising flour
1 teaspoon ground
    mixed spice
95g soft light brown sugar
3 medium eggs
200g (1–2 large) cooking
    apples
45ml milk

For the crumble topping
30g plain flour
20g caster sugar
20g unsalted butter,
    at room temperature

For the custard
    buttercream
100g unsalted butter,
    at room temperature
190g icing sugar
20g custard powder
30ml milk

You will need
900g/2lb loaf tin
baking paper
large piping bag

Preheat the oven to 180°C/160°C fan/gas mark 4. Grease the loaf tin with a little butter and line with a sheet of baking paper.

Put the butter in a large bowl with the flour and mixed spice and use your fingers to rub together until you have a breadcrumb-like consistency. Stir in the light brown sugar, then beat in the eggs, one at a time.

Peel and core the apples, and chop into 1cm cubes. Stir the apples and milk into the mixture until well combined.

Spoon the mixture into the prepared loaf tin and bake in the centre of the oven for 45–55 minutes. The loaf is cooked when a skewer inserted into the centre comes out clean. Leave the loaf to cool completely in the tin and leave the oven on.

While the cake is baking, prepare the crumble topping. Put the flour and sugar in a bowl with the butter. Rub together with your fingers until the mixture resembles a crumble. Line a baking tray with a sheet of baking paper and sprinkle the crumble onto the tray. Once the loaf is out of the oven, bake the crumble mixture for 20 minutes, or until golden. Remove from the oven and leave to cool.

Once the cake and crumble topping have cooled, make the custard buttercream. Beat the butter in a bowl until smooth, then gradually add the icing sugar and continue beating until light and smooth. Combine the custard powder with 25ml of milk in a small bowl. Add the custard mix to the buttercream and beat everything together. If the icing is a little stiff, add another teaspoon of milk.

Spoon the buttercream into a large piping bag and snip around 2cm off the end. Remove the loaf from the tin and use a sharp knife to slice it horizontally into two layers, cutting gently as it will be delicate. Pipe half the buttercream onto the base layer of the sponge in 2cm peaks.

Sprinkle half the crumble topping onto the buttercream (you may need to crumble it between your fingers) and sandwich with the other sponge. Pipe the rest of the buttercream on top of the sponge and sprinkle with the remaining crumble.

TOP TIP
To make it easier to fill the piping bag with buttercream, put the bag into a tall glass or mug while you spoon in the icing.

COCONUT & LIME LOAF

A bright and refreshing citrus bake. A tropically fragrant coconut sponge cake infused with lime zest and juice. Tangy lime syrup is drizzled over the cake before it's topped with a luscious mascarpone icing and a bright sprinkling of lime zest. This makes a delicious alternative to lemon drizzle cake and gives a satisfying kick of tropical flavour.

Serves 10–12

175g unsalted butter, softened
175g caster sugar
3 medium eggs, beaten
175g plain flour
1 teaspoon baking powder
grated zest and juice of 1 lime
80g desiccated coconut

For the syrup
grated zest and juice of 2 limes
120g caster sugar

For the icing
200g mascarpone
75g icing sugar
grated zest of 1 lime, to decorate

You will need
900g/2lb loaf tin
baking paper

Preheat the oven to 180°C/160°C fan/gas mark 4. Grease the loaf tin with a little butter and line with a sheet of baking paper.

Beat together the butter and sugar in a bowl until light and fluffy. Add the beaten eggs, followed by the plain flour and baking powder, and mix together until smooth.

Add the lime zest and juice to the mixture and stir through. Add the coconut and give a final stir.

Pour the mixture into the loaf tin and bake for 40–50 minutes, or until a skewer inserted into the centre comes out clean.

Meanwhile, for the syrup, combine the lime zest and juice with the sugar in a bowl. As soon as the loaf comes out of the oven, use a skewer to pierce holes all over it. Spoon your syrup over the loaf, letting it absorb the liquid. Leave to cool completely in the tin, then remove from the tin and transfer to a plate.

For the icing, beat the mascarpone in a bowl until softened, then mix in the icing sugar. Spread the icing over the top of the cake and finish with a sprinkle of lime zest to decorate.

TOP TIP
Pour all of the lime syrup slowly over your loaf; there may seem to be too much, but this is what gives the cake a perfect texture, and a tangy citrus flavour.

LEMON DRIZZLE LOAF

A mouthwatering, zesty sponge loaf cake drizzled with a tangy lemon syrup and filled with a light, delicate Swiss meringue buttercream. The loaf is topped with a drizzle of white, lemony icing. This is a refreshing, flavourful bake, just perfect with a cuppa.

Serves 10

110g unsalted butter,
  softened
165g caster sugar
2 medium eggs, beaten
195g plain flour
1 teaspoon baking powder
½ teaspoon salt
grated zest of 2 lemons
110ml milk

For the syrup
50g caster sugar
juice of 1 lemon

For the Swiss meringue
  buttercream
40g caster sugar
1 medium egg white
80g unsalted butter,
  softened
60g icing sugar
juice of ½ lemon

For the icing
60g icing sugar
juice of ½ lemon
2 teaspoons roasted
  flaked almonds

You will need
900g/2lb loaf tin
baking paper
small piping bag

Preheat the oven to 180°C/160°C fan/gas mark 4. Grease the loaf tin with a little butter and line with a sheet of baking paper.

Beat together the butter and sugar in a bowl until light and fluffy. Add the eggs, then the flour, baking powder and salt and stir everything together until well combined.

Add the lemon zest and milk and mix well, scraping down the sides of the bowl and beating until everything is combined.

Pour the mixture into the prepared loaf tin and bake for 45–55 minutes, or until a skewer inserted into the centre comes out clean. Take the loaf out of the oven and put the tin on a wire rack. Pierce holes all over the loaf with a skewer.

In a small bowl, mix together the caster sugar and the lemon juice. Spoon this onto your loaf while it is still hot, allowing it to seep in and be absorbed. Leave the loaf to cool completely in the tin, then remove from the tin and transfer to a plate. Use a sharp knife to slice the loaf horizontally into two layers, cutting gently as it will be delicate.

Start preparing your Swiss meringue buttercream. Make sure your bowl and whisk are clean, as any grease or debris will make the meringue collapse. Position a heatproof bowl over a pan of lightly simmering water, making sure the bowl does not touch the water. Put the sugar in the bowl along with the egg white and whisk until the sugar has dissolved. Take off the heat and keep whisking until soft peaks form and the bowl has cooled. The mixture should stand up in peaks when you lift the whisk; this may take a few minutes. Gradually add pieces of the butter, whisking after each addition. Add the icing sugar and lemon juice and continue to whisk until you have a smooth, thick buttercream.

Spoon the buttercream into the piping bag and snip around 5cm off the end. Pipe three rows of buttercream peaks down the centre of the base layer of the loaf. Very carefully sandwich the top half of the loaf on top.

For the icing, put the icing sugar in a clean bowl. Gradually add the lemon juice, mixing after each addition until you have a thick, glue-like consistency. Use a spoon to drizzle the icing over the top of your loaf, then sprinkle over the flaked almonds.

TEA LOAF

A delightful apricot and sultana tea loaf appealingly drizzled with a thick, sweet white icing and decorated with vivid crushed pistachios. This fragrant, fruity loaf would be a tasty addition to a picnic, or to enjoy on a long country walk.

Serves 10

225ml boiled water
1 x everyday tea bag
90g dried apricots, chopped
110g sultanas
100g soft light brown sugar
200g self-raising flour
2 medium eggs, beaten
100g icing sugar
10g pistachios, finely chopped, to decorate

You will need
900g/2lb loaf tin
baking paper

Pour the boiled water into a mug and brew the tea bag for 3 minutes, then discard the tea bag.

Put the dried apricots, sultanas and sugar in a medium bowl and pour the brewed tea over the top. Stir briefly to dissolve the sugar, then cover and leave for at least 1 hour.

Preheat the oven to 150°C/130°C fan/gas mark 2. Grease the loaf tin and line with a sheet of baking paper.

Add the flour and eggs to the tea-infused mixture and mix thoroughly until smooth.

Pour the mixture into the prepared tin and bake for 85–95 minutes. It is ready when a skewer inserted into the centre comes out clean. Remove from the oven and leave the cake to cool completely in the tin. When cool, remove from the tin and transfer to a wire rack.

Put the icing sugar in a bowl and add 1–1½ tablespoons cold water. Mix to form a smooth icing, then drizzle over the cooled cake. Sprinkle the chopped pistachios over the top of the iced cake to decorate.

TOP TIP
For a stronger tea flavour, soak the fruit for a few hours or even overnight, leaving the tea bag in the mixture (discard before using).

MUFFIN
TIN
RECIPES

BLUEBERRY MUFFINS

An enticing batch of sweet and juicy blueberry coffee-shop muffins, topped with a satisfyingly crunchy granola made of oats, cinnamon, crisp demerara sugar and brittle shards of pecan nuts. A perfect muffin for a weekend breakfast treat, or to pop into your lunchbox.

Serves 18

115g unsalted butter, melted and cooled
200g caster sugar
3 medium eggs, beaten
250ml milk
310g plain flour, plus 1 extra teaspoon
1 teaspoon baking powder
1 teaspoon bicarbonate of soda
¼ teaspoon salt
¼ teaspoon vanilla extract
200g blueberries
15g demerara sugar

For the granola topping
75g oats
½ teaspoon ground cinnamon
20g demerara sugar
30g pecan nuts, finely chopped
20g unsalted butter, melted and cooled

You will need
2 x 12-hole muffin tins
18 muffin cases

Preheat the oven to 220°C/200°C fan/gas mark 7. Line the muffin tins with the cases. If you only have one tin, you will need to bake in two batches.

In a large bowl, mix together the melted butter, sugar and eggs. Add the milk and mix again.

Fold in the 310g flour, baking powder, bicarbonate of soda, salt and vanilla until all the ingredients are just combined – be careful not to over mix.

In a separate bowl, coat the blueberries in the extra teaspoon of flour; this will stop them sinking to the bottom of the muffins. Fold all the blueberries into the muffin mixture, then divide the mixture into the muffin cases, filling the cases to the rim of the tin.

To make the granola topping, combine the oats, ground cinnamon, demerara sugar and pecans in a bowl with the melted butter.

Sprinkle the granola mix over the top of the muffins then sprinkle the tops with the 15g demerara sugar. Bake for 5 minutes, then reduce the oven temperature to 190°C/170°C fan/gas mark 5 and continue to bake for a further 15–20 minutes. Check one of the muffins using a skewer – if it comes out clean, the muffins are done. Leave the muffins to cool completely in the tins.

LEMON & POPPY SEED MUFFINS

A dozen light, zesty citrus muffins with a slight poppy seed crunch and liberally drizzled with a tangy lemon syrup. The muffins are delicately iced with a thick, lemon-scented, white icing. Possibly the best breakfast food ever, and absolutely legendary with a cup of strong coffee.

Serves 12

grated zest of 1 and juice
  of 2 lemons
220g caster sugar
335g self-raising flour
1 teaspoon baking powder
20g poppy seeds
2 large eggs
250ml milk
60g unsalted butter

For the syrup
50g granulated sugar
juice of ½ lemon

For the icing
125g icing sugar
juice of ½ lemon

You will need
12-hole muffin tin
small piping bag

Preheat the oven to 200°C/180°C fan/gas mark 6. Grease the holes of the muffin tin generously with butter.

In a large bowl, mix together the lemon zest with the sugar, flour, baking powder and poppy seeds.

In a separate bowl, beat the eggs gently and stir in the milk. Melt the butter in a pan or in the microwave and add to the milk/egg mixture. Add the lemon juice and mix again, then pour into the flour mixture and stir gently until just combined. Spoon or pour equal measures into each hole of the prepared muffin tin.

Bake for 20–25 minutes until lightly browned and well risen. Insert a skewer into a couple of the muffins to test if they are done (the skewer should come out clean). Leave to cool in the tin for a few minutes before carefully transferring to a wire rack. Pierce holes all over the muffins with a skewer.

Make the lemon syrup by combining the sugar and lemon juice in a small bowl. Drizzle over the muffins while they are still warm, then leave them to cool completely.

For the icing, combine the icing sugar with the lemon juice in a small bowl until it is the consistency of toothpaste. If the mixture is too thick, add a tiny amount of water, stir again and continue adding more water as necessary. Spoon the icing into the piping bag, snip a small piece off the end and decorate the tops of the muffins as desired.

TOP TIP
It's important not to over mix muffin batter, so the mixture should be only just combined – lumpy batter is fine!

BANANA CARAMEL MUFFINS

A delicately flavoured banana muffin filled with a gooey caramel sauce and topped with a smooth caramel-flavoured buttercream, a drizzle of bitter dark chocolate and a crunchy banana chip. Easy to accidentally eat more than one, so watch out.

Serves 12

130g unsalted butter
3 large or 4 small over ripe bananas (300g peeled weight)
2 large eggs, beaten
200g plain flour
160g caster sugar
2 teaspoons baking powder
1 teaspoon ground cinnamon
½ teaspoon bicarbonate of soda
pinch of salt
60ml milk
25g dark chocolate chips
30g banana chips

For the caramel
120g granulated sugar
pinch of salt
35g unsalted butter
35ml milk

For the buttercream
125g unsalted butter, softened
205g icing sugar

Preheat the oven to 180°C/160°C fan/gas mark 4. Line the muffin tin with the cases.

Melt the butter in a pan or microwave and leave to cool for a few minutes. Mash the bananas with a fork in a large bowl. Add the cooled melted butter and beaten eggs to the bananas and mix until combined. Gradually add the flour, sugar, baking powder, ground cinnamon, bicarbonate of soda and salt, along with the milk, gently folding after each addition.

Divide the mixture evenly between the muffin cases and bake for 20–25 minutes, or until golden brown. Leave to cool for 10 minutes in the tin, then transfer to a wire rack to cool completely. While the muffins are cooling, make the caramel.

For the caramel, put the sugar and salt in a saucepan and stir in 2 tablespoons of water. Put the pan over a medium heat but do not stir the mixture as this will cause it to crystallise. If the mixture starts to cook unevenly, lift the pan and gently swirl the contents. When the caramel is a golden amber colour (which should take about 7–9 minutes), add the butter and stir until melted.

Take the pan off the heat, add the milk and stir again. Be cautious as the caramel is very hot and will bubble up a little. Once the bubbling has settled, stir until smooth. Transfer to a clean bowl and set aside to cool a little, though don't leave it for too long, as it may begin to solidify.

When the muffins have cooled, use a sharp knife to cut an upturned cone from the centre of each one, about the diameter of a 5 pence piece. Set the cut-out pieces aside. Transfer 1½ tablespoons of caramel to a separate large bowl, then spoon the remaining caramel into the centre of each muffin. Put the cut-out pieces back into the muffins to fill the holes.

To make the buttercream, add the butter to the bowl containing the reserved caramel. Briefly beat the butter and caramel, then gradually add the icing sugar, mixing until pale and smooth. Fill the piping bag with the icing, snip 2–3cm off the end and pipe a generous swirl onto each muffin.

You will need
12-hole muffin tin
12 muffin cases
large piping bag

Put the dark chocolate chips in a heatproof bowl positioned over a pan of simmering water, making sure the bowl does not touch the water. Once melted, drizzle the dark chocolate over each muffin and add a banana chip to finish. These muffins are best served at room temperature.

SPICED BLACKBERRY MUFFINS

A bountiful batch of fragrantly spiced ground almond and blackberry muffins, topped with a sprinkling of demerara sugar to give a treacly, golden, crunchy top. An inspired way to use a glut of gleaming blackberries. As the mix makes so many, these muffins are perfect for sharing with friends and neighbours.

Serves 20

190g unsalted butter,
   melted and cooled
120g caster sugar
150g soft light brown sugar
3 eggs
250g self-raising flour
¾ teaspoon bicarbonate
   of soda
1 teaspoon baking powder
1½ teaspoons ground
   ginger
¾ teaspoon ground
   cinnamon
¼ teaspoon salt
200ml milk
70g ground almonds
25g demerara sugar

For the blackberries
250g blackberries
20g self-raising flour
20g soft light brown sugar

You will need
2 x 12-hole muffin tins
20 muffin cases

Preheat the oven to 190°C/170°C fan/gas mark 5. Line the muffin tins with the cases. If you only have one tin, you will need to bake in two batches.

To prepare the blackberries, halve each blackberry (unless they are very small) and put in a bowl. Sprinkle the flour and sugar over the halved blackberries and stir gently to coat each berry. Set aside.

In a large bowl, combine the melted butter and sugars. Whisk vigorously for 2–3 minutes, until the mixture becomes slightly thicker. Add one egg at a time to the mixture, whisking thoroughly each time.

In a bowl, combine the flour, bicarbonate of soda, baking powder, spices and salt. Fold the dry ingredients and milk gently into the butter mixture, alternating between the two until you have an almost smooth batter (a few lumps are ok).

Add the blackberries and ground almonds to the batter and fold very gently until just combined. Ensure the blackberries remain intact.

Fill each muffin case three-quarters full and sprinkle the top of each with demerara sugar. Bake for 18–20 minutes, until a skewer inserted into one of the muffins comes out clean and the tops are golden and crunchy. Leave the muffins to cool in the tin for 10 minutes, then transfer to a wire rack to cool completely. Serve just warm or cooled with a dollop of créme fraîche.

TOP TIP
To keep the batter light, try not to over mix the batter.

APPLE & PECAN BUNS

A tasty batch of buns, stuffed full of cinnamon and sugar-coated diced apple. These light, airy buns are then sprinkled with a fine crumble of crushed pecan nuts, giving a little added crunch, and drizzled with a glossy white icing. A satisfying bread-based bake, irresistible at any time of day.

Serves 12

250g strong white bread
   flour, plus extra to dust
½ teaspoon salt
95g unsalted butter
150ml lukewarm milk
3g quick yeast
35g caster sugar
200g (1–2 large) cooking
   apples
½ tablespoon ground
   cinnamon
25g dark brown sugar
15g roasted pecan nuts,
   roughly chopped
75g icing sugar

You will need
12-hole muffin tin

Put the flour and salt in a bowl with 45g of butter and rub together with your fingers until you have a fine breadcrumb-like mixture.

Add the milk, yeast and 15g of caster sugar to the flour mixture and combine using a wooden spoon until a dough is formed, then use your hands to bring it together. Dust a clean worktop with a little flour, then put the dough onto the floured surface and knead for 5 minutes. Return the dough to the bowl and cover with cling film, then leave to rise somewhere warm for 60–90 minutes, until it has roughly doubled in size.

While your dough is rising, peel, core and chop the apples into 1cm chunks. Put into a saucepan along with the remaining caster sugar, ground cinnamon and 2 tablespoons of water. Put the pan over a medium heat and cook for around 5 minutes, or until the apples just start to soften, stirring occasionally to prevent burning. Remove from the heat and set aside.

Grease the holes of the muffin tin generously with butter. When your dough has risen, remove it from the bowl and put on a sheet of baking paper dusted with flour. Roll out the dough into a rectangular shape (25 x 40cm), around 1cm thick.

Beat the remaining butter in a bowl to soften, then carefully spread over the rolled-out dough. Spoon the apple mixture over the dough, distributing it evenly to the edges. Scatter the brown sugar over the apples, breaking up any large chunks of sugar with your fingers. Tightly roll up the dough lengthways into a sausage shape, using the paper to help if necessary.

Cut the roll into 12 even slices, then put each slice flat into a hole of the tin and sprinkle the chopped pecans over each bun. Loosely cover the tin with cling film and leave the buns somewhere warm to prove for around 30 minutes, or until they expand in the tin.

Preheat the oven to 180°C/160°C fan/gas mark 4. Bake the buns for 20–25 minutes, or until golden brown. Leave the buns in the tin for 5 minutes to cool slightly before transferring to a wire rack.

While the buns are baking, put the icing sugar in a bowl and gradually add around 3 teaspoons of water until you have a thick, smooth icing. Drizzle the icing all over the buns while they are still hot. The buns are best enjoyed slightly warm.

TOP TIP
Make sure the dough is left to rise in a place that is warm enough, otherwise it may not double in size.

TOFFEE APPLE MUFFINS

A dozen apple and toasted walnut muffins, delicately flavoured with mixed spice. The muffins are drizzled with a light, sticky toffee sauce and studded with chewy fudge pieces. A comforting, autumnal bake, perfect for Halloween or Bonfire Night celebrations.

Serves 12

50g walnuts, chopped
200g plain flour
2 teaspoons baking
    powder
½ teaspoon bicarbonate
    of soda
1 teaspoon ground
    mixed spice
pinch of salt
½ teaspoon vanilla extract
160g caster sugar
2 apples
2 medium eggs,
    lightly beaten
130g unsalted butter,
    melted and cooled
4 tablespoons milk
40g toffee pieces, diced,
    to decorate

For the icing
85g soft light brown sugar
20g unsalted butter
1 tablespoon milk

You will need
12-hole muffin tin
12 muffin cases

Preheat the oven to 180°C/160°C fan/gas mark 4. Line the muffin tin with the cases.

Put the walnuts on a baking tray and roast for 5 minutes, then remove from the oven and set aside to cool.

Put the flour, baking powder, bicarbonate of soda, mixed spice, salt and vanilla in a bowl and stir in the sugar to combine.

Peel, core and chop the apples into 1cm cubes and put them in a large bowl. Add the eggs and cooled melted butter and stir to combine. Fold in the dry ingredients along with the walnuts and milk and give everything a final mix.

Divide the batter evenly between the muffin cases, filling them to the top of the tin. Bake for 20–25 minutes – they are ready when they spring back when gently pressed. Leave to cool for 15 minutes in the tin, then transfer to a wire rack to cool completely.

To make the icing, combine the sugar, butter and milk in a small pan over a low heat and simmer gently for a minute. Drizzle over the muffins and push the toffee pieces into the tops of the muffins to decorate.

THANKS

I'd like to say a few thank-yous to the people who have made our first recipe book possible.

Firstly, the whole Bakedin team, who have helped shape every recipe in this book, from the production team through to the sales team and everyone in between. You all work phenomenally hard and care passionately about our products. I'm extremely proud to be part of the Bakedin family with you all.

My friends and family, many of whom have supported me financially, picked me up when times have been hard and cheered me on when times have been good. There's too many to mention, but if I've roped you in to helping out at markets, packing up kits, labelling boxes or delivering flyers, then thank you!

My two co-founders, Anna and Elaina, who played a big part in getting the business to the point where we were ready to take investment, and filled the early years with so many good memories.

My brother Patrick for taking a leap of faith and leaving a stable job to join me in the business at a difficult time and become my rock, helping to grow Bakedin to where it is today.

Ian and David for being two of our first shareholders and giving me valuable business advice as part of the Bakedin board in the early years.

All of our investors, many of whom are close family and friends, who could see the potential for the business and the positive difference it could make to society. You gave us financial stability when we needed it most and the Baking Club would not be here without you.

To Jon and his whole team at Jon Croft Editions for helping us turn an idea into this beautiful book, and being an absolute pleasure to work with.

A special thank-you goes to the late Michel Roux, who helped us create a lot of the recipes in this book. He was a truly inspirational man, widely regarded as the greatest chef this country has ever seen, and we were very fortunate to have had him as part of our business and in our lives.

Finally, a massive thank-you to all our Baking Club members, past and present. You are the reason the club not only exists, but thrives. Many of you have been with us since the first-ever box and continue to support us allowing the club to go from strength to strength.

First published in Great Britain by Jon Croft Editions in 2020

info@joncrofteditions.com
www.joncrofteditions.com

ISBN: 9780993354021

Printed in Slovenia for Latitude Press Ltd

Reprinted December 2020

Publisher Jon Croft
Commissioning Editor Meg Boas
Project Editor Emily North
Art Direction and Design Peter Moffat
  and Anika Schulze
Photography Lauren Mclean
Food Stylist Vicki Smallwood
Copyeditor Rachel Malig
Proofreader Susan Low
Indexer Zoe Ross